JOH[...]

THE

ACCEPTABLE

SACRIFICE

THE BLESSING OF A BROKEN
AND CONTRITE HEART

EDITED FOR TODAY BY JAMES PITMAN

FAITHESSENTIALS

CLC

PUBLICATIONS

Fort Washington, PA 19034

The Acceptable Sacrifice
FaithEssentials Edition

Published by CLC Publications

U.S.A.
P.O. Box 1449, Fort Washington, PA 19034
www.clcpublications.com

UNITED KINGDOM
Kingsway CLC Trust
Unit 5, Glendale Avenue, Sandycroft, Flintshire, CH5 2QP
www.equippingthechurch.com

Printed in the United States of America

ISBN (paperback): 978-1-61958-328-3
ISBN (e-book): 978-1-61958-329-0

Unless otherwise noted, Scripture quotations are taken from the King James Version of the Bible, which is in the public domain.

Italics in Scripture quotations are the emphasis of the author or editor.

Contents

THE

ACCEPTABLE

SACRIFICE

FAITHESSENTIALS

Editor's Preface

John Bunyan, the author of this book, is known and loved worldwide for his book *The Pilgrim's Progress*. It is easy, for those of us who have read it, to visualize Pilgrim carrying his heavy load, his burden of sin, on the way to the Celestial City to find relief. When I first came across this book by John Bunyan, I was struck by the simplicity and beauty of the idea that a broken and contrite heart is what God really desires. Having long struggled with my "burden"—my natural tendency toward sin—I easily identified with Bunyan's Pilgrim, and with David of Psalm 51 as he cried out to God for mercy. Like David, I have grieved over the depravity of my nature. Like David, I have begged God to wash me clean and give me a pure heart. Like David, I have pled with God not to reject me, but to give me the desire and power to obey Him.

But wait—the sacrifices God desires are a humble, broken, and repentant heart?

And He is the one who does the breaking?

Yes! The breaking comes from the work of the Holy Spirit in each sinner—sometimes by a whisper or a word, and sometimes by a hurricane. And that broken, repentant heart is a heart that God treasures—above any other sacrifice or payment we could offer him on our own.

The Acceptable Sacrifice was originally published in 1688, the same year of Bunyan's death. We have made slight editorial changes to Bunyan's text to clarify meaning where he used words or phrases that are unknown today; but we have done our best to retain the flavor of Bunyan, to remind the reader that this is a unique voice from the past.

As Bunyan says in this text, "God will break ALL hearts for sin, either here to repentance and happiness, or in the world to come to condemnation and misery." Oh, may God's people have soft and humble hearts that are an acceptable sacrifice to God.

James Pitman

Postscript—Mr. Pitman wishes to acknowledge the assistance of Alexandra Green in the editorial process, and to point out that the "Editor's Notes" at the end of the book are not his, but are from the 1692 edition.

Introduction

*The sacrifices of God are a broken spirit: a broken
and a contrite heart, O God, thou wilt not despise.*

—Psalm 51:17

Psalm 51 is called David's penitential psalm—
and rightly so, because it reveals the genuine
sorrow David had for his horrible sin of defiling
Bathsheba and slaying Uriah her husband (see
2 Samuel 11–12).

Many workings of the heart this poor man
had, as soon as conviction fell upon his spirit.
First he cries out for mercy, then he confesses
his heinous offenses, then he grieves over the
depravity of his nature. Sometimes he cries out
to be washed and sanctified, and then again he is
afraid that God will cast him away from his presence and take his Holy Spirit utterly from him.

And thus he goes on till he comes to verse
17, and there he stays, finding in himself that

heart and spirit which God did not dislike: "The sacrifices of God," he says, "are a broken spirit;" as if he is saying, "I thank God I have that." "A broken and a contrite heart," says he, "O God, thou wilt not despise;" as if he should again say, "I thank God I have that."

Let us look at verse 17 in more detail.

1

The Many Workings
of the Heart

The words of Psalm 51:17 consist of an assertion ("The sacrifices of God are a broken spirit") and a demonstration of that assertion ("[Because] a broken and a contrite heart, O God, thou wilt not despise").

In the assertion there are two things presented for our consideration: first, that God considers a broken spirit as a sacrifice; and second, that it is to God something which goes beyond all sacrifices. "The sacrifices of God are a broken spirit."

The demonstration of this is plain: for that heart God will not despise. "A broken and a contrite heart, O God, thou wilt not despise."

From which I draw this conclusion: That a spirit rightly broken, a heart truly contrite, is to God an excellent thing. It is something that goes beyond all external duties whatsoever; for that is what is intended by the phrase "the sacrifices," because it answers to all sacrifices which we can offer to God; yes, it serves in the room of all. All our sacrifices without this are nothing; this alone is all.

There are four things that are very acceptable to God.

First is the sacrifice of the body of Christ for our sins. You read of this in Hebrews 10, where you find it preferred to all burnt offerings and sacrifices; it is this that pleases God; it is this that sanctifies and makes the people acceptable in the sight of God.

Second is the genuine love for God, counted better than all sacrifices or external parts of worship. "And to love him [the Lord thy God] with all the heart, and with all the understanding, and with all the soul, and with all the strength, and to love his neighbor as himself, is more than all whole burnt offerings and sacrifices" (Mark 12:33).

Third is to walk in holiness, humbly and obediently, towards and before God. "Hath the LORD as great delight in burnt offerings and sacrifices, as in obeying the voice of the LORD? Behold, to obey is better than sacrifice, and to hearken than the fat of rams" (1 Sam. 15:22).

And this in our text is the **fourth**: "The sacrifices of God are a broken spirit: a broken and a contrite heart, O God, thou wilt not despise."

But note by the way, that this broken, this broken and contrite heart, is thus excellent only to God: "O God," says he, "*Thou* wilt not despise [it]." By which it is implied that the world does not have esteem or respect for such a heart, or for one that is of a broken and a contrite spirit. No—no—a man or a woman that is blessed with a broken heart, is so far off from getting the same esteem from the world, that they are thought of as burdens wherever they are or go. Such people carry with them abuse and uneasiness: in carnal families, they are like David was to the king of Gath, troublers of the house (see 1 Sam. 21:12–15).

Their sighs, their tears, their day and night groans, their cries and prayers, put all the carnal family out of order.[1] Thus you have them browbeaten by some, condemned by others, and their company fled from and deserted by others. But note the text, "A broken and a contrite heart, O God, thou wilt not despise," but rather accept; for not to despise is with God to esteem and set a high price upon.

2

The Excellency of
a Broken Heart

Here we will demonstrate in several ways that a broken spirit, a spirit *rightly* broken, a heart *truly* contrite, is to God an excellent thing.

First, we see that this is evident from the comparison, "Thou desirest not sacrifice; else would I give it: thou delightest not in burnt offering. The sacrifices of God are a broken spirit" (Ps. 51:16–17). Notice that God rejects both sacrifices and offerings: that is, all Levitical ceremonies under the law and all external works under the gospel, but He accepts a broken heart. It is therefore clear by this, even if nothing else were to be said, that a heart rightly broken, a heart truly contrite, is to God an excellent thing.

Such a heart is placed above all sacrifice—and yet those sacrifices were the ordinances of God and things that He commanded. A broken spirit is placed above them all; a contrite heart goes beyond them—yes, beyond them—when put all together. Oh, brethren, a broken and a contrite heart is a truly excellent thing.

Second, a broken spirit is of greater esteem to God than is either heaven or earth.

> Thus saith the LORD, The heaven is my throne, and the earth is my footstool; where is the house that ye build unto me? and where is the place of my rest? For all those things hath mine hand made, and all those things have been, saith the LORD: but to this man will I look, even to him that is poor and of a contrite spirit, and trembleth at my word. (Isa. 66:1–2)

Mark this: God says He has made all these things, but He does not say that He will look to them or delight in them. But let a brokenhearted sinner come before Him—He ranges throughout the world to find just such a one—and He says, "to this man will I look" (66:2). Such a man is to Him of more value than heaven or earth. "They shall perish" (Heb. 1:11) and vanish away, but this man continues: he, as is presented to us in another place, "abideth forever" (1 John 2:17).

"To this man will I look," or "with this man will I be delighted" as it often reads. "Thou hast ravished my heart, my sister, my spouse" says Christ to His humble-hearted one. "Thou hast ravished my heart with one of thine eyes" (Song of Sol. 4:9). Here you see that He looks and is ravished; He looks and is captivated. "The king is held in the galleries" (7:5) or captivated by His beloved, with the dove's eyes of His beloved, as He is with the contrite spirit of His people. But it is not the same for Him with respect to heaven or earth; He holds them more lightly. They are stored up for fire on the day of judgment, as it says in Second Peter 3:7, but the broken in heart are His beloved, His jewels, and He is taken with them.

Again, what I have said about this is plainly the truth of God, that a brokenhearted sinner, a sinner with a contrite spirit, is of more esteem with God than is either heaven or earth. He says He has made them, but He does not say He will look to them. He says they are His throne and footstool, but He does not say they have taken or captivated His heart. No, it is those that are of a contrite spirit that do this.

But there is found even more in the words "To this man will I look": that is, *For this man will I care, around this man will I camp, I will put this man under my protection*. This is what "to look to" someone sometimes signifies, and I take this to be the meaning here (as it is in Prov. 27:23; Jer. 39:12, 40:4).

"The LORD upholdeth all that fall, and raiseth up all those that be bowed down" (Ps. 145:14). The brokenhearted are included in this number; and He cares for, camps around, and has set His eyes upon such a person for good. This, therefore, is a second demonstration to prove that the man that has his spirit rightly broken, his heart truly contrite, is of great esteem with God.

Third and further, God not only prefers such a person over heaven and earth, but He loves and desires that person intimately, as a companion; He must dwell with them; He must live with him that is of a broken heart, with such as are of a contrite spirit. "For thus saith the high and lofty One that inhabiteth eternity, whose name is Holy; I will dwell in the high and holy place, with him also that is of a contrite and humble spirit" (Isa. 57:15).

Behold here both the majesty and gracious-ness of the high and lofty One; His majesty, in that He is exalted and inhabits eternity. Truly this consideration is enough to make the brokenhearted man creep into a mousehole to hide himself from such a majesty! But behold His heart, His loving and gracious mind: "I also will dwell with the one that has a broken heart, with him that is of a contrite spirit; that is, the person that I would converse with; that is, the one with whom I will cohabit; that is, the person," says God, "that I will choose for my companion." For the desire to dwell with someone means all these things; and truly, of all the people in the world, none are acquainted with God, none understand what communion with Him is and what His teachings mean, but those that have a broken and contrite heart. He "is nigh unto them that are of a broken spirit," it says in Psalm 34:18.

These are the ones Psalm 14 speaks of, where it says that the Lord looked down from heaven "to see if there were any that did understand and seek God" (14:2). He looked to find somebody in the world with whom He might converse, for there are none but the brokenhearted that either understand, or that can come to Him. God, I might say, is "forced" to break men's hearts before He can make them willing to cry out to Him, or to be willing that He should have any part of them. The rest shut their eyes, stop their ears, withdraw their hearts, or say to God, "Depart from us" (Job 21:14). But the broken in heart can understand and seek God. They have the time, the will, and the understanding and are therefore a fit person for God. There is room in this person's house, in this one's heart, in their spirit, for God to dwell, for God to walk, and for God to set up a kingdom.

Here, then, is suitableness. "Can two walk together," says God, "except they be agreed?" (Amos 3:3). The brokenhearted desire God's company—"O when wilt thou come unto me?" (Ps. 101:2) they say. The brokenhearted love to hear God speak and talk to them—"Make me to hear joy and gladness; that the bones which thou hast broken may rejoice" (51:8). But here lies the glory, in that the high and lofty One, the God that inhabits eternity and that has a high and holy place for His habitation, should choose to dwell with, and to be a companion of, the broken in heart and those who are of a contrite spirit. Yes, this is great comfort for such a one.

Fourth, not only does God prefer such a heart above all sacrifices, esteem such a person above heaven and earth, and desire to truly know him, but He reserves for him His chief comforts and lets him drink of His heart-reviving and soul-cherishing medicines. He says that He dwells with the person of contrite heart to revive, support, and comfort them—"to revive the spirit of the humble, and to revive the heart of the contrite ones" (Isa. 57:15). The broken-hearted man is a fainting man; he has his fears, his times of doubt; he often struggles with pain and anxiety; he must be steadied with his cup and comforted with food or he doesn't know what to do. He pines away in his iniquity; nothing can really make him well but the comforts of almighty God. It is with such a person that God will dwell—"To revive the spirit of the humble, and to revive the heart of the contrite ones."

God has medicines, but they are to comfort those that are cast down (see 2 Cor. 7:6); and such are the brokenhearted. Those that are well do not need the physician (see Mark 2:17). Those who are broken in spirit stand in need of medicine, and physicians are most highly esteemed by those who have been sick, rather than the healthy. This is one reason why God is so little thought of by those who have not been made sick by the wounding stroke of God. But when a person is wounded, has his bones broken, or is made sick and is at the mouth of the grave, who is more highly esteemed than an able physician? What is as highly desired as the medicines, comfort, and suitable supplies of the skillful physician in those cases? And thus it is with the brokenhearted; he needs (and God has prepared for him) plenty of the comforts and medicines of heaven, to heal and relieve his sinking soul.

Such a person lies waiting for consolation, sick and despondent under the sense of sin and the heavy wrath of God; and God says they shall be refreshed and revived by His healing balms. Yes, His medicines are designed for them; He has broken their hearts, He has wounded their spirits, so that He might prepare them to relish His reviving comfort. For indeed, as soon as He has broken them, His compassions churn around within Him and will not let Him abide further afflicting. Ephraim was one of these—as soon as God had smitten him, look at His heart and how it reaches towards him. "Is Ephraim my dear son?" He says, as if to say that he is so. "Is he a pleasant child?" as if to say that he is so. "For since I spake against him, I do earnestly remember him still: therefore my bowels are troubled for him; I will surely have mercy upon him, saith the LORD" (Jer. 31:20). This therefore is another demonstration.

Fifth, as God prefers such a contrite heart and esteems the one that has it above heaven and earth; as He covets intimacy with such a person and prepares for him his balm and comfort; so when He sent His Son Jesus into the world to be a Savior, He gave Him a special charge to take care of people like this. Yes—that was one of the main reasons He sent Him down from heaven, anointed for His work on earth. "The Spirit of the Lord is upon me," He says, "because he hath anointed me to preach the gospel to the poor; he hath sent me to heal the brokenhearted" (Luke 4:18; Isa. 61:1). Now, that this is meant of Christ is confirmed by His own lips, for He took the book in His hand when He was in the synagogue at Nazareth and read this very passage to the people. He then told them that this Scripture was fulfilled that very day in their hearing (see Luke 4:21).

But see, these are the souls whose welfare is arranged in the heavens. God planned out their salvation, their deliverance, and their health before his Son came down from there. Does this not demonstrate, then, that a broken-hearted man, that a person of a contrite spirit, is greatly esteemed by God? I have often been surprised that David gave Joab and his warriors the command to deal gently with that young rebel Absalom, his son (see 2 Sam. 18:5). But when I think that God, the high God against whom we have sinned, would so quickly give his Son a command, a charge, to take care of, to bind up, and heal the broken in heart; this is something which can never be sufficiently admired or wondered at by men or angels.

And as He was commissioned, so He acted, as is seen clearly in the parable of the man who fell among thieves. He went to him with compassion, poured into his wounds wine and oil; he bandaged him up, set him on his own animal and took him to an inn. He gave the innkeeper a charge to look after him, with money in hand and a promise at his return to pay him for any further expenses (see Luke 10:30–35). Behold, then, the care of God which He has for the broken in heart. He has given a charge to Christ his Son to look after them and to bind up and heal their wounds. See also the faithfulness of Christ, who does not hide, but enters straight into his commission as soon as he begins his ministry. "He healeth the broken in heart, and bindeth up their wounds" (Ps. 147:3).

And behold again into whose care a broken heart and a contrite spirit has put this poor person; he is under the care of God—the care and cure of Christ. If a person was sure that his disease had put him under the special care of the king and the queen, he still could not be sure of living—he might die even under their sovereign hands. Ah, but here is a man in the favor of God, and under the hand of Christ is to be healed; under whose hand none has ever died due to a lack of skill and power; and so this man must live. Christ has a commission not only to bind up his wounds, but to heal him. He Himself has so expounded on His commission, that the person with a broken heart and contrite spirit must not only be taken in hand, but healed; healed of his pain, grief, sorrow, sin, and fears of death and hellfire. Then He adds that He must give unto such a one "beauty for ashes, the oil of joy for mourning, the garment of praise for the spirit of heaviness," and must "comfort all that mourn" (Isa. 61:2–3). This is

His charge—the brokenhearted are put into His hand, and He Himself has said that He will heal him. "I have seen his ways, and will heal him; I will lead him also, and restore comforts unto him, and to his mourners. . . . and I will heal him" (Isa. 57:18–19).

Sixth, as God prefers such a contrite heart and so esteems the man that has it; as He desires his company, has provided for him His medicines, and given a charge to Christ to heal him, so He has promised in conclusion to save him. He "saveth such as be of a contrite spirit" (Ps. 34:18).

And this is the conclusion of all; for to save a man is the pinnacle of all special mercy. "He saveth such as be of a contrite spirit." To save is to forgive; for without forgiveness of sins we cannot be saved. To save is to preserve one in this miserable world, and to deliver one from all those devils, temptations, snares, and destructions that would, were we not kept and preserved by God, destroy us, body and soul, forever. To save is to bring a man, body and soul, to glory, and to give him an eternal mansion in heaven, that he may dwell in the presence of this good God, and the Lord Jesus, and to sing to Them the songs of his redemption for ever and ever. This is what it is to be saved; nor can anything less than this complete the salvation of the sinner. Now this is the destiny of the one with a broken heart and a contrite spirit. "He saveth such as be contrite of spirit." He saves them! This is excellent!

But do the broken in spirit believe this? Can they imagine that this is to be the end that God has designed them for when they are faced with the day in which He began to break their hearts? No, no; alas! They think quite the contrary. They are afraid that this is but the beginning of death and a sign that they will never see the comforting face of God—neither in this world nor that which is to come. And so they cry out, "Cast me not away from thy presence" (Ps. 51:11). For indeed, when one's heart is being broken, there comes a visible appearance of the wrath of God, and a charge of sin-guilt from heaven to the conscience. This is dreadful to our reason; for it cuts the soul down to the ground, for "a wounded spirit who can bear?" (Prov. 18:14).

It seems to this person, then, that this is the beginning of hell—the first step down to the pit; when in reality, this breaking is nothing but the beginnings of love and that which makes way for life. The Lord kills before He makes alive; He wounds before His hands make whole. Yes, He does the first, so that or because He wants to do the other. He wounds because His purpose is to heal. "He maketh sore, and bindeth up: he woundeth, and his hands make whole" (Job 5:18). His design or plan is the salvation of the soul. He disciplines, He breaks the heart of every son whom He receives, and what sorrow for the one whose heart God does not break.

And so I have proved what at first I asserted, that a spirit rightly broken and a heart truly contrite, is to God an excellent thing. First, this is evident as it is better than sacrifices, than all sacrifice. Secondly, the man that has it is more highly esteemed by God than heaven or earth. Third, God desires such a person to dwell with Him as an intimate companion. Fourth, He reserves for them His medicines and spiritual comforts. Fifth, He has given His Son a charge, a commandment, to take care that the broken-hearted be healed, and He is resolved to heal them. Sixth and finally, that the brokenhearted and those of a contrite spirit shall be saved and dwell eternally with God.

3

What Is a Broken Heart
and a Contrite Spirit?

I come now to show you what a broken heart
and a contrite spirit is. This must be done,
for in the discovery lies both the comfort for
those who have it and the conviction for those
who do not. Now, that I may do this better, I
will propound and speak on these four things.
First, I must show you what a heart is that is
not broken—that is not contrite. Second, I
will show you how the heart is broken and
made contrite. Third, I will show you what
a broken and contrite heart is, and fourth,
I will give you some signs of a broken and
contrite heart.

What is a heart like which is not broken or contrite?

- The heart, before it is broken, is hard, stubborn and obstinate against both God and the salvation of the soul (see Zech. 7:12; Deut. 2:30, 9:27).

- It is a heart full of evil imaginations and darkness (see Gen. 18:12; Rom. 1:21).

- It is a heart that is deceitful and subject to be deceived, especially about the things of eternal significance (see Isa. 44:20; Deut. 11:16).

- It is a heart that gathers sin and vanity to itself rather than anything that is good for the soul (see Ps. 41:6, 94:11).

- It is an unbelieving heart, and one that will turn away from God to sin (see Heb. 3:12; Deut. 17:17).

- It is a heart that is not prepared for God nor for the reception of His holy Word (see 2 Chron. 12:14; Ps. 78:8; Acts 7:51).

- It is a double heart and deceptive; it will pretend to serve God, but will lean to the devil and sin (see Ps. 12:2; Ezek. 33:31).

- It is a proud heart; it loves to be uncontrolled, even if the controller is God Himself (see Ps. 101:5; Prov. 16:5; Mal. 3:13).

- It is a heart that will make room for Satan but will resist the Holy Spirit (see Acts 5:3, 7:51).

- To sum up, "It is deceitful above all things, and desperately wicked;" so wicked that none can know it (see Jer. 17:9).

That this is the condition of the heart before it is broken, and even worse than I have described it to be, is sufficiently seen by the whole course of the world. Is there any man whose heart has not been broken and whose spirit is not contrite, that according to the Word of God deals honestly with his own soul? It is a primary characteristic of a right heart that it is sound in God's statutes and honest (see Ps. 119:18; Luke 8:15). But alas! How few people, however honest they are to others, are honest about the condition of their own soul!

What causes the heart to be broken and the spirit made contrite, and how does it happen?

God uses His Word to break one's heart. "Is not my word like as a fire? saith the Lord; and like a hammer that breaketh the rock in pieces?" (Jer. 23:29). The rock, in this text, is the heart, which in another place is compared to a stone that is harder than flint (see Zech. 7:11–12). This rock, this stony heart, is broken and made contrite by the Word. But it only becomes contrite when the Word is used by God like a fire and a hammer to break and melt it. No man can break the heart with the Word; no angel can break the heart with the Word; only God can do this by His own mighty power from heaven. This made Balaam go without a heart rightly broken and truly contrite even though he was rebuked by an angel. It allowed the Pharisees to die in their sins, even though they were rebuked and admonished to turn from them by the Savior of the world. Therefore, though the Word is the instrument with which the heart is broken, it will not be broken with the Word until that Word is managed by the might and power of God Himself.

This made the prophet Isaiah, after long preaching, cry out that he had labored in vain. It made him cry for God "to rend the heavens and come down," so that the rocky mountains (or rocky hearts) might be broken and melt at His presence (see Isa. 49:4, 64:1–2). For he found by experience, that no effective work could be done unless the Lord put His hand to it. This is often intimated in the Scriptures, where it says that when the preachers preached effectively to the breaking of men's hearts, "the Lord working with them" (Mark 16:20), "the hand of the Lord was with them" (Acts 11:21), and other similar statements.

Now when the hand of the Lord is with His Word, then it is mighty. It is "mighty through God to the pulling down of strong holds" (2 Cor. 10:4). It is sharp as a sword in the soul and spirit. It sticks like an arrow in the hearts of sinners, causing people to fall at His feet for mercy (see Heb. 4:12). Then it is, as was said before, like a fire and a hammer to break this rock in pieces (see Ps. 110:3).

When it stands by itself and is not empowered from heaven, it is called the Word only, the Word barely, or as if it was only the word of men (see 1 Thess. 1:5–7). The Word of God, when only in a man's hand, is like a father's sword in the hand of an infant; this sword, though well pointed and ever so sharp on the edges, is not able to conquer a foe and make an enemy fall and cry out for mercy, because it is only in the hand of a baby. But now, let the same sword be put into the hand of a skillful father—and God is both skillful and able to manage His Word—and then the sinner, and the proud helpers too, are both made to bow and submit themselves. And so I say, though the Word is the instrument, yet by itself it does no saving good to the soul; the heart is not broken nor the spirit made contrite by it. It only works death, and leaves men in the chains of their sins, bound for eternal condemnation (see 2 Cor. 2:15–16).

But when accompanied by the mighty power of the Spirit of God, then the same Word is like the roaring of a lion, or the piercing of a sword, like a burning fire in the bones, or a hammer that dashes all to pieces (see Jer. 25:30; Amos 1:2, 3:8; Acts 2:37; Jer. 20:9; Ps. 29:3–9). So then, whoever has heard the Word preached but has not heard the voice of the living God therein, has not yet had their hearts broken, nor their spirits made contrite for their sins.

How does the Word bring about a broken heart and a contrite spirit? When it exposes the sinner and his sin, convincing him that he has been found out. This is how it was with our first father, Adam. When he had sinned, he sought to hide himself from God. He hid among the trees of the garden, and there he shrouded himself. But still, not thinking himself secure, he covered himself with fig leaves and then lay quiet. *Now*

God shall not find me, he thinks, *and nor know what I have done*. But listen! He "hears the voice of the Lord God walking in the garden." And now, Adam, what are you going to do? Why, he continues to skulk and hides his head, seeking yet to lie undiscovered; but behold, the Voice cries out, "ADAM!" and now he begins to tremble. "Adam, where art thou?" says God; and now Adam is forced to answer (see Gen. 3:7–11).

But the voice of the Lord God does not leave him here. No, it now begins to inquire after his doings, and to unravel what he had wrapped together and covered, until it lays him bare and naked in his own sight before the face of God.

This, then, is what the Word does when managed by the arm of God. It finds out—it singles out the sinner. The sinner finds that it exposes his sins. It unravels his whole life, strips him, and lays him naked in his own sight before the face of God. Neither the sinner nor his wickedness can be hidden and covered any longer, and now the sinner begins to see what he never saw before.

Another example of this is David, the man of our text. He sins—he sins grossly—and hides it. Yes, he seeks to hide it from the face of both God and man. Then Nathan is sent to preach a message to him, first in general by way of a parable, then through special and particular application to David himself. When Nathan only preached in general, David stood as right in his own eyes as if he had been as innocent and as harmless as any man alive. But God had a love for David and therefore commands his servant Nathan to bring the message home, not only to David's ears, but to David's conscience. "Thou art the man," says Nathan, and now David must fall. "I have sinned," David confesses, and his heart is broken and his spirit made contrite, as both this psalm and our text shows (see 2 Sam. 12:1–13).

A third example is that of Paul (Saul)—he had heard many a sermon in his life and had become a respected teacher himself. He was more zealous than many of his equals, but his heart was never broken, nor his spirit made contrite, until he heard God in heaven, in the Word of God, making inquiry about his sins. "Saul, Saul, why persecutest thou me?" asks Jesus. And then Saul can no longer stand; his heart breaks and he falls to the ground. He trembles, then cries out, "Who art thou, Lord?" and "Lord, what wilt thou have me to do?" (Acts 9:4–6).

So the Word works effectively when it exposes the sinner and his sin, and convinces him that it has found him out. Only I must add a caution here, for not every operation of the Word upon the conscience is saving; nor does all conviction end in the saving conversion of the sinner. It is necessary then, that the sinner must not only see the evil of his ways, but his heart must be brought over to God by Christ. And this brings me to the third thing.

What kind of heart is one that has been broken and made contrite?

To answer this question, we must first understand two things. First, what is meant by the word *broken*, and second, what is meant by the word *contrite*.

For the word *broken*, I think of it as being more than a heart that is merely *troubled*. I take it to be a heart that is *disabled* as to its former actions, even as a man whose bones are broken is disabled from running, leaping, wrestling, or other physical activity. Therefore, that which was called a broken heart in our text, he then refers to as broken bones in verse eight. "Make me," he says, "to hear joy and gladness, that the bones which thou hast broken may rejoice" (Ps. 51:8).

Now why is the breaking of the heart compared here to the breaking of bones? Because when bones are broken, the physical man is disabled from doing what he was previously able to do with ease. In the same way, when the spirit is broken, the inward man is disabled as to the vanity and folly he delighted in formerly. He loses the strength and former vigor he had to engage in vain and sinful paths.

This is what it is to have the heart *broken*— to have it lamed and disabled from following the course of life it formerly took, because of a sense of God's wrath due to sin. And to show that this work is no easy thing, but only comes with great trouble to the soul, it is compared to the breaking of bones, the burning of bones with fire, and more. (see Ps. 51:8; Lam. 1:13; Ps. 6:2; Prov. 17:22).

Now, what is meant by the word *contrite*? A contrite spirit is a repentant spirit; one deeply grieved and sorrowful for the sins it has committed against God, and for the damage done to the soul. This is the meaning in those places where a *contrite* spirit is mentioned; as in Psalm 34:18; Isaiah 57:15, 66:2.

Like a man who by his own foolishness has broken an arm or leg and is heartily sorry that he was so unwise as to be engaged in such foolish activity, so is he whose heart is broken with a sense of God's wrath due to his own sin. He has deep sorrow in his soul and is greatly repentant that he could ever be such a fool and by his rebelliousness bring himself and his soul so much suffering. Such a person freely calls his sin his greatest folly. "My wounds stink, and are corrupt," says David, "because of my foolishness" (Ps. 38:5). And again, "O God, thou knowest my foolishness; and my sins are not hid from thee" (69:5).

Whatever men say with their lips, if their hearts have not yet been broken, they cannot conclude that sin is a foolish thing. Hence it says, "The foolishness of fools is folly" (Prov. 14:24). That is, the foolishness of some people is that they take pleasure in their sins; for their sins are their foolishness, and the folly of their soul lies in their living with this foolishness.

But the man whose heart is broken cannot be like this, no more than the one with broken bones can rejoice that he is wanted to play a football match. Hence, to hear others talk foolishly actually brings grief to those whom God has wounded. As it says, their words are "like the piercings of a sword" (Prov. 12:18). This is what I take to be the meaning of these two words, a *broken* and a *contrite* spirit.

What are the signs of a broken heart and a contrite spirit?

First, *a brokenhearted man is a sensitive man*; that is, he has been brought to his senses concerning his soul. All others are dead, senseless, and without true feeling of what the brokenhearted man is now sensitive to.

1. He sees himself to be that which others are ignorant of—that he is not only a sinful man, but a man by nature in the bondage of sin. Poisoned by bitterness and sin was how Peter expressed it to Simon the Sorcerer, and every man in his natural state is poisoned by sin. He was shaped in it, conceived in it, and is possessed by it, and that possession infected his whole soul and body (see Ps. 51:5; Acts 8:23). He sees this and he understands it. David says, "There is no soundness in my flesh" (Ps. 38:3), and Solomon suggests that a plague or affliction is in the very heart (see 1 Kings 8:38). But not everyone perceives this.

David even says that the wounds caused by his foolishness stank and festered (see Ps. 38:5). But one whose heart was never broken has no understanding of this. The brokenhearted man *sees*—he sees his sickness, he sees his wound. "When Ephraim saw his sickness, and Judah saw his wound" it says in Hosea 5:13. He sees it to his grief and to his sorrow.

2. He feels what others have no sense of—he feels the arrows of the Almighty, and that they stick fast in him (see Ps. 38:2). He feels how sore and sick, by the smiting of God's hammer upon his heart to break it, his poor soul is made. He feels a burden intolerably lying upon his spirit (see Hos. 5:13). "Mine iniquities," he says, "are gone over mine head: as a heavy burden they are too heavy for me" (Ps. 38:4). He also feels the heavy hand of God upon his soul—a thing unknown to carnal men. He feels pain, being wounded, even such pain as others cannot understand, because they are not broken. "My heart," David says, "is sore pained within me." Why so? "The terrors of death are fallen upon me" (Ps. 55:4). The terrors of death cause pain—pain of the highest nature; hence that which is

here called "pains" is in another place called "pangs" (Isa. 21:3).

You know broken bones can cause pain, strong pain—pain that will make a man or woman groan "with the groanings of a deadly wounded man" (Ezek. 30:24). Soul pain is the sorest pain, in comparison to which the pain of the body is a very tolerable thing (see Prov. 18:14). Here is soul pain, here is heart pain; here we are speaking of a wounded, broken spirit; wherefore this is pain to be felt to the sinking of the whole man, neither can any relieve it but God. There is death in this pain, death forever, without God's special mercy. This pain will bring the soul to a standstill, and this the brokenhearted man feels. "The sorrows of death," said David, "compassed me, and the pains of hell gat hold upon me, I found trouble and sorrow" (Ps. 116:3). Yes, I'll agree with you, poor man, you found trouble and sorrow indeed; for the pains of hell and sorrows of death are the most intolerable pains and sorrow. But this is a familiar experience to the man who has his heart broken.[2]

3. As he sees and feels, so he hears that which augments his woe and sorrow. You know, if a man has his bones broken, he not only *sees* and *feels*, but also often *hears* things that only increase his grief—that his wounds are incurable, that his bone is not set properly, that there is danger of a gangrene, that he may die because of his neglect. These are the voices of doom that haunt the house of one that has his bones broken. A brokenhearted man knows what I mean by this; he hears that which makes his lips quiver, and he seems to feel rottenness enter into his bones; he trembles within himself, and wishes that he may hear joy and gladness, that the bones, the heart, and the spirit which God has broken, may rejoice (see Hab. 3:16; Ps. 51:8). He thinks he hears God say, the devil say, his conscience say, and all good men say, whispering among themselves, "There is no help for him in God" (3:2). Job heard this, David heard this, Heman heard this; and this is the common sound in the ears of the brokenhearted.

4. The brokenhearted smell what others cannot smell. Sin never smelled so to any man alive

as it smells to the brokenhearted. Infected wounds will stink, but there is no stink like that of sin to the brokenhearted man. His own sins stink, and so do the sins of all the world to him. Sin is like carrion—it has a stench, the worst of smells (see Ps. 38:5)—yet some men like it. But none are offended with the scent of sin but God—and the brokenhearted sinner. "My wounds stink, and are corrupt," he says, "both in God's nostrils and my own." But who smells the stink of sin? Not the carnal world; they, like carrion crows, seek it, love it, and eat it as a child eats bread. "They eat up the sin of my people," God says, "and they set their heart on their iniquity" (Hos. 4:8). They do this because they do not smell the nauseous scent of sin. Whatever is nauseous to the smell cannot be palatable to the taste. The brokenhearted man finds sin nauseous, and cries out, "It stinks!" They also think at times that the smell of fire, fire and brimstone, is upon them, so sensitive are they of the wages of sin.

5. The brokenhearted is also a tasting man. Wounds, if sore and very painful, sometimes alter the taste of a man; they make him think

his meat and his drink have a bitter taste to them. How many times do the poor people of God (the only ones who know what a broken heart means) cry out that gravel, wormwood, gall, and vinegar, was made their meat (see Lam. 3:15–16, 19)? This gravel, gall, and wormwood is the true temporal taste of sin; and God, to make them loathe it forever, feeds them with it till their hearts both ache and break with it. Wickedness tastes pleasant to the world; hence it is said they feed on ashes, and on the wind (see Isa. 44:20; Hos. 12:1). Lusts, or anything that is vile and worthless, the carnal world thinks is enjoyable—as is seen most notably in the parable of the prodigal son: "He would fain have filled his belly," said our Lord, "with the husks that the swine did eat" (Luke 15:16). But though the brokenhearted man may appreciate these things, because of the anguish of his soul he abhors all manner of dainty meat (see Job 33:19–20; Ps. 107:17–19).

Thus I have shown you one sign of a brokenhearted man: he is a sensitive man, with all the senses of his soul awakened; he can see, hear, feel, taste, and smell as no one else can do.

I come now to another sign of a broken and contrite man.

Second, *a brokenhearted man is a very sorrowful man.* Just as being sensitive is natural, it is also natural for one in pain, for one who has his bones broken, to be a grieved and sorrowful man. He is not one of the jolly ones of his generation; nor can he be, for his bones, his heart, is broken.

1. He is sorry that he feels and finds in himself a depraved nature; I told you before he is sensitive to it, he sees it, he feels it; and here I say he is sorry for it. It is this that makes him call himself a wretched man; it is this that makes him loathe and abhor himself; it is this that makes him blush—blush before God and be ashamed (Rom. 7:24; Job 42:5–6; Ezek. 36:31). He finds by nature no form nor comeliness in himself, but the more he looks in the mirror of the Word, the more unhandsome, the more deformed he perceives sin has made him. Not everyone sees this, therefore not everyone is sorry for it; but the broken in heart sees that he is corrupted by sin, marred, full of lewdness and naughtiness. He sees that in him, that

is, in his flesh, dwells no good thing, and this makes him sorry—yes, it makes him heartsick. A man that has his bones broken finds he is spoiled, marred, disabled from doing as he would and should, at which he is grieved and made sorry.

Many are sorry for actual transgressions, because they often cause them shame before others; but few are sorry for the defects that sin has made in nature, because they do not see those defects themselves. A man cannot be sorry for the sinful defects of nature till he sees they have rendered him contemptible to God; nor is it anything but a sight of God that can make him truly see what he is, and so be heartily sorry for being so. "Now mine eye seeth thee," says Job, "Wherefore I abhor myself" (Job 42:5–6). "Woe is me! for I am undone," says the prophet, "for mine eyes have seen the King, the LORD of hosts" (Isa. 6:5). And it was this that made Daniel say, "my comeliness was turned in me into corruption" (Dan. 10:8), for he had now the vision of the Holy One. Visions of God break the heart because, by the sight the soul then has of His perfections, it sees its own infinite and unspeakable disproportion, because of the vileness of its nature.

Suppose a company of ugly, uncomely, deformed persons dwelt together in one house; and suppose they never saw anyone other than themselves—never saw a physically fit, attractive, and well-formed person. They would not be capable of comparing themselves with anyone but themselves, and would not be sorry for their physical defects. But bring them out of their house, where they have been shut up by themselves, and let them view the splendor and perfections of beauty in others, and they will be sorry and disappointed with their defects.

This is the case spiritually: humans are marred, spoiled, corrupted, and depraved by sin, but they may dwell by themselves in the dark; they see neither God, nor angels, nor saints, in their excellent nature and beauty: and therefore they are apt to count their own uncomely parts their ornaments and their glory. But let them see God, see saints, or the ornaments of the Holy Ghost, and themselves as they are without them, and then they cannot fail to be affected with and sorry for their own deformity.

When the Lord Christ put forth but little of his excellency before his servant Peter's face, it raised up the depravity of Peter's nature before him to his great confusion and shame; and made him cry out to Him in the midst of his fellow disciples, "Depart from me, for I am a sinful man, O Lord" (Luke 5:8).

This therefore is the cause of a broken heart, even a sight of divine excellencies, and a sense that I am a poor, depraved, spoiled, defiled wretch; and this sight having broken the heart, begets sorrow in the brokenhearted.

2. The brokenhearted is a sorrowful man; for that he finds his depravity of nature strong in him, putting itself forth to oppose and overthrow what his changed mind prompts him to do. "When I would do good," said Paul, "evil is present with me" (Rom. 7:21). Evil is present to oppose, to resist, and make headway against the desires of my soul. The man that has his bones broken, may have yet a mind to be industriously occupied in a lawful and honest calling; but he finds, by experience, that an infirmity attends his present condition that strongly resists his good endeavours; and at this he shakes his

head, makes complaints, and with sorrow of heart he sighs and says, "I cannot do what I want to do" (see Rom. 7:15; Gal. 5:17). He is weak, feeble; not only depraved, but by that depravity deprived of any ability to put good motions,[3] good intentions, and desires into execution, to completeness. "Oh," he says, "I am ready to give up, my sorrow is continually before me!"

You must know that the brokenhearted loves God, loves his soul, loves good, and hates evil. Now, for such a one to find in himself an opposition and continual contradiction to this holy passion, it must cause sorrow—godly sorrow, as the apostle Paul calls it. For such are made sorrowful in a godly way. To be sorry that your nature is depraved with sin, and that through this depravity you are deprived of the ability to do what the Word and your holy mind prompts you to do, is to be sorry in a godly way. For this sorrow works in you that which you will never have cause to repent of; no, not for eternity (see 2 Cor. 7:9–11).

3. The brokenhearted man is sorry for those breaches that, by reason of the depravity of

his nature, are made in his life and conversation. And this was the case of the man in our text. The vileness of his nature had broken out and defiled his life, making him, at this point, degraded in his conduct. This was what altogether broke his heart. He saw in this that he had dishonored God, and that cut him. "Against thee, thee only, have I sinned, and done this evil in thy sight" (Ps. 51:4). He saw in this that he had caused the enemies of God to open their mouths and blaspheme; and this cut him to the heart. This made him cry, "I have sinned against the LORD" (2 Sam 12:13). This made him say, "I will declare mine iniquity; I will be sorry for my sin" (Ps. 38:18).

When a man is determined to do something, when his heart is set upon it, as the brokenhearted determines to glorify God, an obstruction to that determination, the spoiling of this work, makes him sorrowful. Hannah coveted children, but could not have them, and this made her "a woman of a sorrowful spirit" (1 Sam. 1:15). A brokenhearted man would be well inwardly, and do that which is well outwardly; but he feels, he finds, he sees he is prevented, at least in part. This makes him sorrowful; in this he groans earnestly, being burdened with his flaws (see 2 Cor. 5:1–3). You know one with broken bones has many flaws, and is more aware of them than any other man (as was said before); this makes him sorrowful, and makes him conclude, "I shall go softly all my years in the bitterness of my soul" (Isa. 38:15).

Third, *the man with a broken heart is a very humble man*. True humility is a sign of a broken heart. Hence, brokenness of heart, contrition of spirit, and humbleness of mind, are put together. "To revive the spirit of the humble, and to revive the heart of the contrite ones" (Isa. 57:15).

To follow our comparison, suppose a man, while healthy, stout, and strong, who fears and cares for no man, breaks a leg or an arm. His courage is quelled; far from bullying other men, he is afraid of every little child that simply tries to touch him. Now he may call on the most feeble person he knows to help him and handle him gently. Now he has become a child in courage, a child in fear, and humbles himself as a little child.

Thus it is with a man who is of a broken and contrite spirit. Time was, indeed, he could argue, even argue with God Himself, saying, "What is the Almighty, that we should serve him?" (Job 21:15); or, "It is vain to serve God: and what profit is it that we have kept his ordinance . . . ?" (Mal. 3:14). But now his heart is broken; God has wrestled with him, and given him a fall, to the breaking of his bones, his heart; and now he crouches, cringes, and begs God to not only do him good, but do it with tender hands. "Have mercy upon me, O God," said David; "according unto the multitude of thy tender mercies, blot out my transgressions" (Ps. 51:1).

He stands, as he sees, not only his need of mercy, but of the tenderest mercies. God has several sorts of mercies, some more rough, some more tender. God can save a man, and yet the man may have a dreadful way to heaven! This the brokenhearted sees, and this the brokenhearted dreads, and therefore pleads for the tenderest sort of mercies; and here we read of His gentle dealing, that He is very pitiful, and deals tenderly with His people.

But the reason for such expressions no one knows but the brokenhearted, who has sores, running sores, stinking sores; who is in pain, and therefore desires to be handled tenderly. Thus God has broken the pride of his spirit, and humbled the loftiness of the man. And his humility appears in a number of ways.

1. *In his thankfulness for natural life.* He reckons when he goes to bed at night that God, like a lion, will tear him to pieces before the morning light (see Isa. 38:13). There is no judgment that has fallen on others that he does not count himself worthy of being swallowed up by. "My flesh trembleth for fear of thee, and I am afraid of thy judgments" (Ps. 119:120). But perceiving a day added to his life—that in the morning he is still on this side of hell—he can't help but take notice of it, and acknowledge it as a special favor, saying, "God be thanked for holding my soul in life till now, and for keeping my life back from the destroyer" (see Job 33:22; Ps. 56:13, 86:13).

Man, before his heart is broken, counts time his own, and therefore spends it lavishly upon every idle thing. His soul is far from fear, because the rod of God is not upon him. But when he sees himself under the wounding hand of God, or when God, like a lion, is breaking all his bones, he humbles himself before God, and falls at His feet. He has learned to count every moment a mercy, and every small morsel a mercy.

2. Now also the smallest hope of mercy for his soul—oh, how precious it is! He had been inclined to consider the gospel as rubbish, its valued promises as stubble, and the words of God as rotten wood. But now, how does he look on the promise? He counts any possibility of mercy more rich and of more worth than the whole world. Now, as we say, he is glad to leap at a crust; now, to be a dog under God's table, or a doorkeeper in His house, is counted better by him than to "dwell in the tents of wickedness" (Ps. 84:10; see also Matt. 15:25–27; Luke 15:17–19).

3. He used to look with scorn upon the people of God, and refused to give them so much as a kindly look; now he admires and bows before them, and is ready to lick the dust off their feet. He would count it his highest honor to be as one of the least of them. "Make me as one of thy hired servants" (Luke 15:19), he says.

4. Now he is, in his own eyes, the greatest fool in nature; for he sees that he has been so mistaken in his ways, and still has little, if

any, true knowledge of God. "Everyone," he says, "has more knowledge of God than I; everyone serves Him better than I" (see Ps. 73:21–22; Prov. 30:2–3).

5. Now his goal is to be but one, though the least in the kingdom of heaven! To be but one, though the least in the church on earth! To be loved, though the least beloved of saints! How high a value he sets upon it!

6. Now, when he talks with God or men, how he debases himself before them! If with God, how does he accuse himself, and load himself with the acknowledgments of his own sinful acts, which he committed in the days when he was the enemy of God! "Lord," said Paul, that contrite one, "I imprisoned and beat in every synagogue them that believe; on thee. And when the blood of thy martyr Stephen was shed, I also was standing by, and consenting unto his death, and kept the raiment of them that slew him" (Acts 22:19–20). Yes, he says, "I punished [the saints] oft in every synagogue, and compelled them to blaspheme; and being exceedingly mad against them, I persecuted them even unto strange cities" (26:11).

Also, when he comes to speak to saints, how he makes himself vile before them! "I am," he says, "the least of the apostles; that am not meet to be called an apostle"; he calls himself "less than the least of all saints, " a blasphemer, a persecutor, injurious, etc. (1 Cor. 15:9; Eph. 3:8; see also 1 Tim. 1:13).

What humility, what self-abasing thoughts, a broken heart produces! When David danced before the ark of God, how did he discover his nakedness to the disliking of his wife? And when she taunted him for what he did, he says, "It was before the LORD, . . . And I will yet be more vile than thus, and will be base in mine own sight" (2 Sam. 6:21–22). The man who has been kindly broken in spirit, who is of a contrite heart, is a lowly, humble man.

Fourth, *the brokenhearted man is a man who sees himself in spiritual things to be poor*. Just as *humble* and *contrite* are put together in the Word, so are *poor* and *contrite*. "But to this man will I look, even to him that is poor, and of a contrite spirit" (Isa. 66:2). And here we still pursue our metaphor. A wounded man, a man with broken bones, considers his condition to be very poor. Ask him how he is, and he answers, "In a very poor condition!"

The spiritual poverty of the brokenhearted is often mentioned in the Word, and they are called by two names to distinguish them from others. They are called "Thy poor," that is, God's poor; they are also called "the poor in spirit" (see Ps. 72:2, 74:19; Matt. 5:3). The man who is poor in his own eyes (and such is the brokenhearted), is aware of his wants. He knows he cannot help himself, and therefore is forced to be content to live by the charity of others. Thus it is in nature, thus it is in grace.

1. The brokenhearted man now knows his need, and he knew it not till now, as one with a broken bone knew of no need of a bone-setter till he knew his bone was broken. His broken bone makes him know it; the pain and anguish makes him know it; and thus it is in the spiritual life. Now he sees that to be poor indeed is to sense his need of the favor of God; for his great pain is a sense of wrath, as has been shown before. And the voice of joy would heal his broken bones (see Ps. 51:8). Two things he thinks would make him

rich: first, a right and title to Jesus Christ, and all His benefits; and second, saving faith in Him. They that are spiritually rich are rich in Him, and in the faith of Him (see 2 Cor. 8:9; James 2:5).

The first of these gives us a right to the kingdom of heaven; the second yields the soul the comfort of it. The brokenhearted man wants the sense and knowledge of his interest in these. That he knows he wants them is plain; but as yet, he knows he has not attained them. Hence he says, "The poor and needy seek water, and there is none, and their tongue faileth for thirst" (Isa. 41:17). There is no water in view—or, at least, none in view for them. Hence David, when he had his broken heart, felt he needed to be washed, purged, made white. He knew that spiritual riches lay there, but he did not as clearly see that God had washed and purged him. Yes, he rather was afraid that all was lost, that he was in danger of being cast out of God's presence, and that the Spirit of grace would be utterly taken from him (see Ps. 51:11). That is the first thing. The brokenhearted is poor, because he knows his need.

2. The brokenhearted is poor, because he knows he cannot help himself to what he knows he needs. The man with a broken arm knows he cannot set it himself. This, therefore, is the second proof that a man is poor; otherwise he is not so. Suppose a man has a need like he never had before; if he can help himself, if he can supply his own needs out of what he has, he cannot be a poor man. Yes, the more he needs, the greater are his riches, if he can supply his own needs out of his own purse.

Those who are poor know their spiritual need, and also know they cannot supply or help themselves. This the brokenhearted knows, therefore he in his own eyes is the only poor man. True, he may have something of his own, but that will not supply his want, and therefore he is a poor man still. "I have sacrifices," says David, "but You do not desire them, therefore my poverty remains" (see Ps. 51:16). Lead is not gold, lead is not currency to a merchant. There is no one who has spiritual gold to sell but Christ (see Rev. 3:18). What can a man do to procure Christ, or procure faith, or love? Yes, he may have more of his own carnal "excellencies" than ever before, but not one penny of it will be of value in a marketplace where grace is the currency. "If a man would give all the substance of his house for love, it would utterly be contemned" (Song of Sol. 8:7).

This the brokenhearted man perceives, and therefore he sees himself to be spiritually poor. True, he has a broken heart, and that is of great esteem with God; but that is not of nature's goodness; that is a gift, a work of God; and that is the sacrifices of God. Besides, a man cannot remain content and at rest with that; the nature of it is but to show him he is poor, and that his need is such that he cannot supply it himself. Besides, there is but little ease in a broken heart.

3. The brokenhearted man is poor, and sees it; he finds he is now unable to live any way else but by begging. David himself became a begger, though he was a king; for he knew, as to his soul's health, he could live no way else. "This poor man cried," he said, "and the LORD heard him, and saved him out of all his troubles" (Ps. 34:6). And this leads me to the fifth sign.

Fifth, *another sign of a broken heart is a crying, a crying out*. Pain, you know, will make one cry. Go to them that have upon them the anguish of broken bones, and see if they do not cry; anguish makes them cry. Crying quickly follows once your heart is broken and your spirit is made contrite.

1. Anguish will make you cry. "Trouble and anguish," David says, "have taken hold on me" (Ps. 119:143). Anguish, you know, naturally leads to crying; and as a broken bone has anguish, a broken heart has anguish. This why the pains of a broken heart are compared to the pangs of a woman in travail (John 16:20–22).

   Anguish will make one cry alone, cry to one's self; and this is called a bemoaning of one's self. "I have surely heard Ephraim bemoaning himself," said God (Jer. 31:18)—that is, being under the breaking, chastising hand of God. "Thou hast chastised me," he says, "and I was chastised, as a bullock unaccustomed to the yoke." This is what the psalmist meant when he said, "I mourn in my complaint, and make a noise" (Ps. 55:2). And why? "My heart is sore pained within me" (Ps. 55:4).

This is a self-bemoaning, bemoaning themselves in secret and secluded places. You know it is common with those who are in anguish, though all alone, to cry out to themselves of their present pains, saying, "Oh, my leg! Oh, my arm! Oh, my stomach!" Or, as the son of the Shunammite, "My head, my head!" (2 Kings 4:19). Oh, the groans, the sighs, the cries that the brokenhearted have, when all alone! They say, *My sins! My sins! My soul! My soul! How I am loaded with guilt! How I am surrounded with fear! Oh, this hard, this desperate, this unbelieving heart! Oh, how sin defiles my will, my mind, my conscience!* "I am afflicted and ready to die" (Ps. 88:15).[4]

If some of you carnal people were to hide behind the chamber door and hear Ephraim when he is at the work of self-bemoaning, you would stand amazed to hear him bewail that sin in himself in which you take delight; and to hear him bemoan his misspending of time, while you spend all your time pursuing your filthy lusts; and to hear him offended with his heart, because it will not better comply with God's holy will, while you are afraid of his Word and ways, and never think yourselves better than when farthest off from God. The unruliness of the passions and lusts of the brokenhearted often make them get into a corner, and thus bemoan themselves.

2. As they thus bemoan themselves to themselves, so they cry out against themselves to others; as is said in one case, "Behold and see, if there be any sorrow like unto my sorrow" (Lam. 1:12). Oh, the bitter cries and complaints that the brokenhearted have, and make to one another! Everyone imagines that their own wounds are deepest, and their own sores more full of anguish and hardest to cure. They say, "If our transgressions and our sins be upon us, and we pine away in them, how should we then live?" (Ezek. 33:10).

Once, while at an honest woman's house, I asked her, after some pause, how she was doing. She said, "Very badly." I asked her if she was sick. She answered, "No."

"What then?" I asked. "Are any of your children ill?" She told me no.

"What?" I said. "Is your husband amiss, or do you go back in the world?"

"No, no," she said, "but I am afraid I shall not be saved." And she broke down with a heavy heart, saying, "Ah, Goodman Bunyan! Christ and a pitcher; if I had Christ, though I went and begged my bread with a pitcher,[5] it would be better with me than I think it is now!"

This woman had her heart broken; she wanted Christ; she was concerned for her soul. Very few women, especially rich ones, count Christ and a pitcher better than the world, their pride, and their pleasures. This woman's cries are worthy to be recorded; it was a cry that carried in it, not only a sense of the want, but also of the worth of Christ. This cry, "Christ and a pitcher," made a melodious noise in the ears of the very angels!

But as I say, few women cry out this way; few are so in love with their own eternal salvation as to be willing to part with all their lusts and vanities for "Christ and a pitcher."

Good Jacob also was this way; yes, he vowed it should be so: "And Jacob vowed a vow, saying, If God will be with me, and will keep me in this way that I go, and will give me bread to eat, and raiment to put on, So that I come again to my father's house

in peace; then shall the Lord be my God"
(Gen. 28:20–21).

3. As they bemoan themselves and make their
complaints to one another, so they cry to
God: "O lord God," said Heman, "I have
cried day and night before thee" (Ps. 88:1).
But when did he do this? Why, when his soul
was full of trouble, and his life drew near to
the grave (see 88:3). Or, as it says elsewhere,
"Out of the depths have I cried unto thee,
O Lord. . . . Out of the belly of hell cried I"
(Ps. 130:1; Jonah 2:2). By such words they
expressed what painful conditions they were
in when they cried.

4. See how God Himself words it: "My pleasant portion," he says, is become "a desolate
wilderness . . . and being desolate it mourneth unto me" (Jer. 12:10–11). And this also
is natural to those whose hearts are broken.
Where does a child go, when it is hurting,
but to its father or mother? Where does it
lay its head, but in their laps? Into whose
bosom does it pour out its complaint? Into
the bosom of a father or mother, because
there is tenderness, there is pity, there is
relief and succor! And thus it is with them

whose bones, whose hearts are broken. It is natural to them; they must cry; they cannot help but cry to Him. "O LORD, heal me," said David, "for my bones are vexed. My soul is also sore vexed" (Ps. 6:2–3). He that cannot cry feels no pain, sees no need, fears no danger, or else is dead.

Sixth, *another sign of a broken heart and a contrite spirit is, it trembles at God's Word.* "To him that is poor, and of a contrite spirit, and trembleth at my word" (Isa. 66:2).

The Word of God is an awful Word to a brokenhearted man. Solomon says that "The king's wrath" and "The fear of a king" is as "the roaring of a lion" (Prov. 19:12, 20:2). By "wrath" and "fear" is meant the authoritative word of a king. And if the word of an earthly king inspires fear, what of the Word of God?

There is a proverb, "The burnt child dreads the fire, the whipped child fears the rod"; in the same way, the brokenhearted fears the Word of God. As a result, those who tremble at God's Word have certain noticeable behaviors—to wit, they keep among the godly; they are self-controlled; they are most apt to mourn, and to stand in the gap, when God is angry; and to turn away His wrath from a people.

It is a sign the Word of God has had place, and is working powerfully, when the heart trembles at it, is afraid, and stands in awe of it. When Joseph's mistress tempted him to lie with her, he was afraid of the Word of God. "How then can I do this great wickedness," he said, "and sin against God?" (Gen. 39:9). He stood in awe of God's Word, did not dare to do it, because he kept in remembrance what a dreadful thing it was to rebel against God's Word.

When old Eli heard that the ark was taken, his very heart trembled within him; for he read by that sad loss that God was angry with Israel, and he knew the anger of God was a great and terrible thing (see 1 Sam. 4:13).

When Samuel went to Bethlehem, the elders of the town trembled; for they feared that he came to them with some sad message from God, and they had experienced the dread of such things before (see 16:1–4).

When Ezra would have a mourning in Israel for the sins of the land, he sent, and there came to him "every one that trembled at the words of the God of Israel, because of the transgressions of those that had been carried away" (Ezra 9:4).

There are, I say, a sort of people that tremble at the words of God, and are afraid of doing anything contrary to them; but only those whose souls and spirits the Word has broken. For the rest, they are resolved to go their own way, whatever God may say. "As for the word that thou hast spoken unto us in the name of the LORD," said rebellious Israel to Jeremiah, "we will not hearken unto thee. But we will certainly do whatsoever thing goeth forth out of our own mouth" (Jer. 44:16–17).

Do you think that these people ever felt the power and majesty of the Word of God to break their hearts? Not really; had that been so, they would have trembled at the words of God; they would have been afraid of the words of God. Whatever God may command some people, they will do what they want. What do they care about God? What do they care about His Word? Neither threats nor promises, punishments nor favors will make them obedient to the Word of God—and all because they have not felt its power; their hearts have not been broken by it.

When King Josiah read in God's Book what punishment God had threatened against rebellious Israel, though he himself was a holy and good man, he humbled himself. He rent his clothes and wept before the Lord, and was afraid of the judgment threatened (see 2 Kings 22; 2 Chron. 34). For he knew what a dreadful thing the Word of God is.

Some men, as I said before, dare do anything, no matter how much the Word of God is against it; but those who tremble at the Word dare not do so. No, they must make the Word their rule for all they do; they must go to the Holy Bible, and there inquire what may or may not be done; for they tremble at the Word.

This, then, is another sign, a true sign, that the heart has been broken: when the heart is made afraid, and trembles at the Word (see Acts 9:4–6, 16:29–30). Trembling at the Word is caused by a belief of what is deserved, threatened, and of what will come, if not prevented by repentance; and therefore the heart melts, and breaks before the Lord.

4

The Necessity that
the Heart Be Broken

I come, in the next place, to speak to this question: What necessity is there that the heart must be broken? Can't a man be saved unless his heart be broken?

I answer (though not presuming to know those secret things which belong only to God), there is a necessity of breaking the heart to bring one to salvation, because a man will not sincerely comply with the means for bringing him to that point until his heart is broken. For,

First. From the moment he comes into the world, a person is as as one dead—dead to spiritual things, to the gospel—and so stupefied, and wholly self-focused, as to be unconcerned with his eternal destiny. Nor can any call or admonition that lacks a heartbreaking power bring him to a due consideration of his present state, and so to an effectual desire to be saved.

God has demonstrated this in many ways. He has threatened people with temporal judgments, and even sent such judgments upon them, over and over, but they will not turn. He says,

> I have given you cleanness of teeth in all your cities. . . . I have withholden the rain from you. . . . I have smitten you with blasting and mildew. . . . I have sent among you the pestilence. . . . I have overthrown some of you, as God overthrew Sodom and Gomorrah . . . yet have ye not returned unto me, saith the LORD. (Amos 4:6–11)

Here is judgment upon judgment, stroke after stroke, punishment after punishment, but it is of no use, unless the heart is broken. Another prophet seems to say that such things, instead of converting the soul, sends it further away. If the heart is broken by such strokes, "Why should ye be stricken any more?" He says; "ye will revolt more and more" (Isa. 1:5).

Man's heart is fenced in; it has grown shameless; it has a skin that, like a coat of mail, wraps it up and encloses it in on every side. Unless this skin, this coat of mail, is cut off and taken away, the heart remains untouched and unconcerned, whatever judgments or afflictions fall upon the body (see Matt. 13:15; Acts 28:27). What I call the coat of mail or the fence of the heart has two great names in Scripture: "the foreskin of your heart" (Deut. 10:16) and the devil's "armour wherein he trusteth" (Luke 11:22).

This coat of mail shields the heart from all gospel doctrine and all legal punishments; nothing can come at the heart till the shield is removed. In order to be converted, the heart is said to be circumcised; that is, this foreskin is taken away and this coat of mail is removed. "[I] will circumcise thine heart," he says, "to love the LORD thy God with all thine heart"—and then the devil's goods are spoiled—"that thou mayst live" (Deut. 30:6).

And now the heart lies open, and the Word will prick, cut, and pierce it; and having been cut, pricked, and pierced, it bleeds, faints, falls, and dies at the feet of God, unless it is supported by the grace and love of God in Jesus Christ.

Conversion begins in the heart; but if the heart is so secured by sin and Satan, as I have said, all judgments are, while that is so, in vain. That is why Moses, after he had made a long recitation of mercy and judgment to the children of Israel, suggested that three great things were lacking to them—"an heart to perceive, and eyes to see, and ears to hear" (see Deut. 29:2–4). Their hearts were not yet touched to the quick, were not awakened and wounded by the holy Word of God, nor made to tremble at its truth and terror.

But before the heart be touched, pricked, and wounded, how can it be thought, however great the danger, that it should repent, cry, bow, and break at the feet of God, and beg for mercy? And yet that is what it must do; for God has ordained and thus appointed it. Men cannot be saved without it. But, I say, can a man spiritually dead, a stupid man, whose heart is past feeling, do this, before he has his dead and stupid heart awakened to see and feel its state and misery without it? But,

Second. From the moment a person comes into the world, no matter how wise he may be in worldly and temporal things, is still a fool as to the spiritual and heavenly. Hence Paul says,

"The natural man receiveth not the things of the Spirit of God: for they are foolishness unto him"—because he is indeed a fool to them—"neither can he know them, because they are spiritually discerned" (1 Cor. 2:14). But how now can this fool be made wise?

Why, wisdom must be put into his heart (see Job 38:36). No one can put it there but God; and how does he put it there, but by making room there for it, by taking away the thing which hinders, which is that folly and madness which naturally dwells there? But how does he take that away but by a severe chastising of his soul for it, until he has made him weary of it? The whip and stripes are provided for the natural fool, and so it is for him that is spiritually so (see Prov. 19:29).

Solomon implies that it is a hard thing to make a fool become wise. "Though thou shouldest bray [grind] a fool in a mortar among wheat with a pestle, yet will not his foolishness depart from him" (27:22). To grind someone in a mortar with a pestle is a dreadful thing; and yet it seems that a whip, a mortar, and a pestle is the way. And if this is the way to make one wise in this world, and if all this will barely succeed, how must the one who is foolish in spiritual things be whipped and beaten, or ground with mortar and pestle, before he is made wise?

Yes, his heart must be put into God's mortar, and must be beaten; it must be ground there with the pestle of the law before it desires to listen to heavenly things. It is a great word in Jeremiah: "Through deceit"—that is, folly—"they refuse to know me, saith the LORD." And what follows? "Therefore, thus saith the LORD of hosts, Behold, I will melt them, and try them"—that is, with fire—"for how shall I do for the daughter of my people?" (Jer. 9:6–7). "I will melt them: I will put them into my furnace, and there I will try them; and there will I make them know me," says the Lord.

When David was under spiritual chastisement for his sin, and had his heart under the breaking hand of God, he said that God would make him know wisdom (see Ps. 51:6). He was in the mortar, in the furnace, he was bruised and melted; yes, his bones, his heart, was breaking, and his folly was departing. Now, says he, "thou shalt make me to know wisdom" (51:6). If I know anything of the way of God with us fools, it is that nothing else will make us wise; a thousand breakings will not make us as wise as we should be.

We say, "Wisdom is not good till it is bought"; and he that buys it, according to the intention of that proverb, usually smarts for it. The fool is wise in his own conceit (see Prov. 26:5, 12); and a double difficulty hounds him before he can be wise indeed. Not only his folly, but his wisdom, must be removed from him; and how shall that be, but by ripping up of his heart by painful conviction, to show him plainly that his wisdom is his folly, and will be his undoing.

A fool loves his folly; he is so in love with it, it is like a treasure to him. Only something truly great can make a fool forsake his folly. Foolish people will not weigh, or consider, or compare wisdom with their folly. "Folly is joy to him that is destitute of wisdom" (15:21). "As a dog returneth to his vomit, so a fool returneth to his folly" (26:11). They are very reluctant, even when driven from their folly, to let it go, to let it depart from them.

This is why it is such a big deal to make someone a Christian; for in this area, *everyone* is a fool—the greatest, the most unconcerned, the most self-willed of all fools—a fool that will not be turned from folly but by the breaking of his heart. David was one of these fools; Manasseh was one of these fools; Saul, otherwise called Paul, was one of these fools; and so was I—and I was the biggest of all.[6]

Third. From the moment a person comes into the world, he is not only a dead man, and a fool, but a proud man also. Pride is one of those sins that first shows itself to children—it grows up with them and mixes itself with all they do; but in adults it lies more deeply hidden in the soul. For the nature of sin is not only to be vile, but to hide its vileness from the soul.

That is why many think they do well when they sin. Jonah thought he did well to be angry with God (see Jon. 4:9). The Pharisees thought they did well when they said that Christ had a devil (see John 8:48). And Paul truly thought that he ought to do many things against, or contrary to, the name of Jesus; which he also did with great madness (see Acts 26:9–10). Sin puffs up men with such pride and conceit that they think they are a thousand times better than they are. Hence they think they are the children of God, when they are the children of the devil (see John 8:41–44); they think they are part of the Christian faith, when they are not—nor do they know what they must have to be so (see Gal. 6:3).

Where does this flow but from pride and self-conceit? The think that their state is good for another world, when they are yet in their sins, and under the curse of God. This pride is so strong and high, yet so hidden within them, that all the ministers in the world cannot persuade them that it is pride, not grace, in which they are so confident. Hence they slight all reproofs, rebukes, threatenings, or admonitions that are pressed upon them, to prevail with them to take heed, that they be not herein deceived.

"Hear ye," says the prophet, "and give ear: be not proud, for the LORD hath spoken. . . . But if ye will not hear it, my soul shall weep in secret places for your pride" (Jer. 13:15, 17). And what was the conclusion? Why, all the proud men stood out still, and maintained their resistance of God and His holy prophet (see 43:1–4).

Nor is there anything that will prevail with these to the saving of their souls, until their hearts are broken. David, after he had defiled Bathsheba, and slain her husband, still boasted himself in his justice and holiness, and would by all means have the man put to death that had but taken the poor man's lamb, when, poor soul, he himself was the great transgressor. But would he believe it? No, he stood vindicating himself as a just man; nor would he be made to fall until Nathan, by authority from God, told him that he was the man he himself had just condemned. "Thou art the man," he said: at which word his conscience was awakened, his heart wounded, and his soul made to fall under the burden of his guilt, at the feet of the God of heaven for mercy (see 2 Sam. 12:1–13).

Ah, pride—that which holds many a man in the chains of his sins. Cursed self-conceit—that which keeps them from believing that their state is damnable. "The wicked, through the pride of his countenance, will not seek after God" (Ps. 10:4). And if there is that much pride in his countenance, how much do you think is in his heart? This is why Job says it is to "hide pride from man," and so to save his soul from hell, that God chastens him with pain upon his bed, until "the multitude of his bones . . . stick out" and "his soul draweth near to the grave and his life to the destroyers" (see Job 33:17–22).

It is a hard thing to take a man off his pride, and make him, instead of trusting in and boasting of his goodness, wisdom, honesty, and the like, to see himself a sinner, a fool—a man that is cruel to his own immortal soul. Pride of heart has a power in it, and is therefore compared to an iron sinew, and an iron chain, by which they are made hard, and with which they are held in that hardness, to oppose the Lord, and drive His Word from their hearts (see Lev. 26:19; Ps. 73:6).

This was the sin of devils, and it is the sin of man, and the sin, I say, from which no man can be delivered until his heart is broken; and then his pride is spoiled, then he will be glad to yield. If a man be proud of his strength or manhood, a broken leg will cripple him; and if a man be proud of his goodness, a broken heart will cripple him; because, as has been said, a broken heart comes by the discovery and charge of sin, by the power of God upon the conscience.

Fourth. From the moment a person comes into the world, he is not only a dead man, a fool, and proud, but also self-willed and headstrong (see 2 Pet. 2:10). A stubborn, ungainly creature is man before his heart is broken. Hence they are so often called rebels, rebellious, and disobedient: they will only do what they want. "All day long," says God, "have I stretched forth my hands to a disobedient and gainsaying people" (Rom. 10:21). And they are compared to a self-willed or headstrong horse, that will, in spite of his rider, rush into the battle. "Every one," says God, "turneth to his course, as the horse rusheth into the battle" (Jer. 8:6). They say, "With our tongue will we prevail, our lips are our own; who is lord over us?" (Ps. 12:4).

They are said to stop their ears, to pull away their shoulder, to shut their eyes, and harden their hearts (see Zech. 7:11–12) "against the words of God, and contemned the counsel of the most high" (Ps. 107:11). They are fitly compared to the rebellious son who would not be ruled by his parents, or to the prodigal, who would have all in his own hand, and remove himself far away from father and father's house (see Deut. 21:20; Luke 15:13). Now for such creatures, nothing will do but violence. The stubborn son must be stoned till he dies; and the prodigal must be famished out of all; nothing else, I say, will do. Their self-willed stubborn heart will not comply with the will of God before it is broken (see Deut. 21:21; Luke 15:14–17). These are they who are said to have "stoutness [arrogance] of heart"; they are said to be far from righteousness, and will remain so until their hearts are broken; for so they must be made to know themselves (see Isa. 9:9–11).

Fifth. From the moment a person comes into the world, he is not only a dead man, a fool, proud, and self-willed, but also a fearless creature. "There is," the text says, "no fear of God before their eyes" (Rom. 3:18). No fear of God! There is fear of man—fear of losing others' favor, love, good-will, help, and friendship. This is seen everywhere. The poor fear the rich, the weak fear the strong, and those that are threatened fear those who threaten!

But when it comes to God, no one fears Him—that is, by nature, no one reverences Him; they neither fear His frowns, nor seek His favor, nor inquire how they may escape His revenging hand that is lifted up against their sins and their souls because of sin. They are afraid of losing little things, but they are not afraid of losing their soul. They "fear not me, saith the LORD" (Mal. 3:5).

How many times are some men put in mind of death by sickness upon themselves, by graves, by the death of others? How many times are they put in mind of hell by reading the Word, by lashes of conscience, and by some who go roaring in despair out of this world? How many times are they put in mind of the day of judgment? As, 1. By God's binding the fallen angels

over to judgment (see 2 Pet. 2:4); 2. By the
drowning of the old world (see 2:5); 3. By the
burning of Sodom and Gomorrah with fire from
heaven (see Jude 7); 4. By appointing a day of
judgment (see Acts 17:31); 5. By appointing a
judge (see 10:42); 6. By reserving their crimes
in records (see Rev. 20:12); 7. By appointing
and preparing of witnesses (see Rom. 2:15); 8.
And by promising, even threatening or resolv-
ing, to call the whole world to His bar, there
to be judged for all which they have done and
said, and for every secret thing (see Matt. 12:36,
25:31–33; Eccl. 11:9, 12:14).

And yet they fear not God! They do not believe these things. These things, to carnal men,
are like Lot's preaching to his sons and daughters
that were in Sodom. When he told them that
God would destroy that place, he seemed unto
them as one that mocked; and his words to them
were as idle tales (see Gen. 19:14). Fearless men
are not won by words; blows, wounds, and kill-
ings are the things that must bring them under
fear. How many struggling fits had Israel with
God in the wilderness? How many times did
they declare that there they did not fear Him?
And they were seldom if ever brought to fear and

dread His glorious name, unless He surrounded them with death and the grave. Nothing but a severe hand will make the fearless fear.

And so, to speak after the manner of man, God is "forced" to go this way with sinners, to save their souls; He even brings them to the mouth of the abyss, within sight of hell and everlasting damnation; and there He must charge them with sin and guilt, to the breaking of their hearts, before they will fear His name.

Sixth. From the moment a person comes into the world, he is not only a dead man, a fool, proud, self-willed, and fearless, but he is a false believer concerning God. No matter how plainly God speaks about Himself, man by nature will not believe His report (see Isa. 53:1). No, they are become vain in their imaginations, and their foolish heart is darkened; they turn the glory of God, which is His truth, into a lie (see Rom. 1:21–25). God says, "I see"; they say, "He does not see"; God says, "I know"; they say, "He does not know" (see Job 22:13–14). God says, "There is none like me"(Isa. 46:9); yet they say, "He is altogether like us" (see Ps. 50:21). God says, "No one shall do good for nothing" (see Eph. 6:8); they say, "It is in vain, and to no profit to serve

Him" (see Job 21:14–15; Mal. 3:14). He says, "I will do good"; they say, "He will neither do good nor evil" (Zeph. 1:12). Thus they falsely believe concerning God; and as for the word of His grace, and the revelation of His mercy in Christ, they secretly imply by their behavior— for a wicked man speaks with his feet (see Prov. 6:13)—that they believe it to be a stark lie, and not to be trusted (see 1 John 5:10).

Now, what shall God do to save these men? If He hides himself and conceals His glory, they perish. If He sends His messengers, and forbears to come to them Himself, they perish. If He comes to them and forbears to work upon them by His Word, they perish: if He works on them, but not effectually, they perish. To work effectually, He must break their hearts, and make them, as men wounded to death, fall at His feet for mercy, or there can be no good done on them; they will not rightly believe until He fires them out of their misbelief, and makes them to know, by the breaking of their bones for their false faith, that He is, and will be, what He has said of Himself in his holy Word.[7] The heart, therefore, must be broken before the man can come to good.

Seventh. From the moment a person comes into the world, he is not only a dead man, a fool, proud, self-willed, fearless, and a false believer, but a great lover of sin; he is captivated, ravished, drowned in the delights of it. Hence the Word says they love sin (see John 3:19), delight in lies (see Ps. 62:4), take pleasure in iniquity, and in them that do it (see Rom. 1:32); that they revel in their own deceivings (see 2 Pet. 2:13), and glory in their shame (see Phil. 3:19).

This is the temper of man by nature; for sin is mixed with and has the mastery of all the powers of his soul. Hence they are said to be captives to it, and to be led captive into the pleasures of it, at the will of the devil (see 2 Tim. 2:26). And you know it is not an easy thing to take one's affections off an object in which they are so deeply rooted, as man's heart is in his sins.

How sad that so many despise all the allurements of heaven, trample upon all the threatenings of God, and discount all the flames of hell, whenever they are given as motives to forsake their sinful delights—they are so fixed upon, so mad for, these beastly idols. Indeed, trying to stop them from going this way, is like trying to prevent the raging waves of the sea from their course, when driven by the mighty winds.

When people are backed into a corner—when their reason and conscience begin to listen to a preacher, or they otherwise come under conviction for their iniquity—how many evasions, excuses, delays, and hiding-holes they use to hide and preserve their sweet sins! And all to the delight of their souls, and their own eternal destruction.

This is why they endeavor to stifle their conscience, to choke conviction, to forget God, to make themselves atheists, to contradict preachers that are plain and honest, and to seek out only those who are like themselves, "Which say to the seers, See not; and to the prophets, Prophesy not unto us right things, speak unto us smooth things, prophesy deceits," and say to honest preachers, "Get you out of the way, turn aside out of the path, cause the Holy One of Israel to cease from before us" (Isa. 30:10–11).

If their conscience and guilt continues to follow them like bloodhounds, expose them in their secret places, and roar against them for their wicked lives, they will flatter, deceive, and lie against their soul, promising to mend, repent, and grow better shortly; and all to toss aside criticism and guilt feelings over their wicked ways, so they can continue to pursue their lusts, pleasures, and sinful delights without disapproval or restraint.

Yes, I have even known some to roar like bears, yell like dragons, and howl like dogs over the weight of guilt, and the lashes of hell upon their conscience for their evil deeds (see Hos. 7:14); yet as soon as their present torments and fears were gone, they returned to their sin—"the dog is turned to his own vomit again; and the sow that was washed to her wallowing in the mire" (2 Pet. 2:22).

Some have tasted of the good Word of God, the joy of heaven, and the powers of the world to come, and yet could not by any or all of these, be made to break their ties to their lusts and sins (see Heb. 6:4–6; Luke 8:13). Oh, Lord! "What is man, that thou art mindful of him?" (Ps. 8:4); "wherein is he to be accounted of?" (Isa. 2:22). They have sinned against You; they love their sins more than You. They are "lovers of pleasure more than lovers of God" (2 Tim. 3:4)!

But now, how shall such a person be reclaimed from this sin? How shall he be made to fall out of love with it? Doubtless it can be by no other means (from what we read in the Word) but by wounding, breaking, and disabling the heart that loves it, and by that means making it a plague and gall unto it. Sin may be made an affliction, and as gall and wormwood to them that love it; but making sin a bitter a thing to such a man cannot be done but by great and difficult means.

I remember some time ago we had in our town a little girl who loved to eat the heads of foul tobacco-pipes, and neither rod nor good words could reclaim her, and make her leave them. So her father took the advice of a doctor, to wean her from them, and it was this: "Take," he said, "a great many of the foulest tobacco-pipe heads you can get, and boil them in milk, and make your daughter drink it up." He did so, and made his little girl drink it up; it became so irksome and nauseous to her stomach, and made her so sick, that she could never abide to meddle with tobacco-pipe heads any more, and so was cured of that habit.

If you love your sin, and neither rod nor good words will as yet reclaim you, take heed! If you wilt not be reclaimed, God will make you a drink of them, which shall be so bitter to your soul, so irksome to your taste, so loathsome to your mind, and so afflicting to your heart, that it shall break it with sickness and grief, till sin becomes loathsome to you. Thus He will do if He loves you; if not, He will allow you to go your own way, and will let you go on with your tobacco-pipe heads!

The children of Israel wanted meat, and felt they must have it; they wept, cried, and murmured because they didn't have meat; yet the bread of heaven they considered to be poor and pitiful stuff (see Num. 11:4–6). Moses told God how the people despised His heavenly bread, and how they longed and lusted to be fed with meat.

"Well," said God, "they shall have meat; they shall have their fill of meat! I will feed them with it; they shall have to the full."

> Ye shall not eat one day, nor two days, nor five days, neither ten days, nor twenty days; But even a whole month, until it come out at your nostrils, and it be loathsome unto you: because ye have despised the LORD. (11:19–20)

He knows how to make loathsome to you that which you have set your evil heart upon.

And He will do so, if He loves you; otherwise, as I said, He will not make you sick of sin by punishing you for your spiritual adultery, but will leave you alone until the Judgment Day, and call you to account for all your sins then. But let us go on.

Eighth. From the moment a person comes into the world, he is not only a dead man, a fool, proud, self-willed, fearless, a false believer, and a lover of sin, but a wild man. He is of the wild olive tree, wild by nature (see Rom. 11:17, 24). So, in another place, man by nature is compared to a wild donkey: "For vain or empty man would be wise, though man be born like a wild ass's colt" (Job 11:12).

Isaac was a figure of Christ, and of all converted men (see Gal. 4:28). But Ishmael was a figure of man by nature; and the Holy Ghost, as to that, said this of him: "And he will be a wild man" (Gen. 16:12). This man was a figure of all carnal men, in their wildness or alienation from God. Hence it is said of the prodigal, at his conversion, that he "came to himself" (Luke 15:17); implying that he was mad, wild, or out of his wits before. I know there is a difference sometimes between being wild and being mad;

yet sometimes one is wild to such a degree that they can rightly be called mad. And this is always true in spiritual things; he that is wild is seen by God as mad, or beside himself, and so not capable, before he is tamed, of minding his own eternal good as he should. There are several characteristics of one who is wild or mad; and they are all found in a carnal man.

1. A wild or mad man gives no heed to good counsel; the frenzy of his head shuts it all out and leads him away from men that are wise and sober. And thus it is with carnal men; good counsel is to them as pearls are that are cast before swine; it is trampled under foot of them, and the man is despised that brings it (see Matt. 7:6). "The poor man's wisdom is despised, and his words are not heard" (Eccl. 9:16).

2. A wild or mad man, if left to himself, will greatly busy himself all his life to accomplish that which, when completed, amounts to nothing. The work, toil, and travail of such a one comes to nothing, except to show that he who did it was out of his mind. David, when pretending to be mad, scribbled upon the gate of the king, as fools do with chalk

(see 1 Sam. 21:12, 13); and all the work of all carnal men in the world is like this. This is such men are said to have "laboured for the wind" (Eccl. 5:16), or for what will amount to no more than if he should "fill his belly with the east wind" (Job 15:2).

3. If you ask a wild or mad man to do anything, he will not follow your directions, but do it after the folly of his own wild fancy—just as Jehu executed the commandment of the Lord. He did it "furiously," in his own madness, and "took no heed to walk in the law of the LORD" (2 Kings 9:20, 10:31). This is what carnal men do, when they meddle with any of God's matters, such as hearing, praying, reading, or professing; they do it according to their own wild fancy; they take no heed to walk after the commands of the Lord.

4. Wild or mad men, if they deck or array themselves with anything, as many times they do, why, the spirit of their wildness or frenzy appears even in the mode and way in which they do it. Either the things themselves which they make use of for that purpose are mere toys and trifles; or if they seem to be better, they are put on after a

bizarre manner, rendering them ridiculous rather than sober, judicious, or wise; and so do natural men array themselves with what they think is acceptable to God. Would someone in his right mind think he could make himself fashionable or acceptable to men by arraying himself in filthy rags, or by painting his face with dung? And yet this is the "finery" of carnal men, when they seek acceptance into the presence of God (see Isa. 64:6; Phil. 3:7–8).

Oh, the wildness, the frenzy, the madness, that possesses the heart and mind of carnal men! They walk according to the course of this world, after that spirit which is in truth the spirit of the devil, which "worketh in the children of disobedience" (Eph. 2:2). But do they believe this? Of course not. They are, by their own account, as other madmen are, the only ones in the world. They are so taken and tickled with their own frantic notions that they deride anything else in the world.

But how is a wild or mad man made sober? Leaving him alone will not do it; giving him good words only will not do it. No, he must be tamed by some means. "He brought down their heart with labour" (Ps. 107:12), or by continual tribulation. The psalmist speaks here of madmen that "sit in darkness and in the shadow of death, being bound in affliction and iron; Because they rebelled against the words of God, and contemned the counsel of the most High" (107:10–11).

This, therefore, is the way to deal with such people, and none but God can so deal with them. They must be taken, they must be separated from others; they must be laid in chains, in darkness, afflictions, and irons; they must be bloodied, half-starved, whipped, purged, and dealt with as mad people are dealt with, until they come to themselves, and cry out in their distresses. And "Then they cried unto the LORD in their trouble, and he saved them out of their distresses. He brought them out of darkness and the shadow of death, and brake their bands in sunder" (107:13–14). This is how God tames the wild, and brings mad prodigals to themselves, and then to Him for mercy.

Ninth. From the moment a person comes into the world, he is not only a dead man, a fool, proud, self-willed, fearless, a false believer, a lover of sin, and a wild man; but a man who has a distaste for the things of God. I said before that unconverted man is such as did not taste things; but now I add that he has a *dis*taste for things; he calls bitter sweet, and sweet bitter; he judges quite wrongly. These people God threatens with a woe: "Woe unto them that call evil good, and good evil; that put darkness for light, and light for darkness; that put bitter for sweet, and sweet for bitter" (Isa. 5:20).

The latter part of this text shows us evidently that the things of God are distasteful to some. They call His sweet things bitter, and the devil's bitter things sweet; and all this is for want of a broken heart. A broken heart has different tastes than a whole or unbroken one. A man with no pain or bodily distress sees no good in the most effective ointment or salve; were it applied to an arm or leg, he says, "Away with these stinking, greasy things!" But lay the same medication where it is needed, and the patient will relish and savor the goodness of them—yes, and will recommend them to others.

Thus it is in the spiritual life. The world does not know the anguish or pain of a broken heart; they say, "Who will shew us any good?" (Ps. 4:6)—that is, better than we find in our amusements, pleasures, possessions, and interests. "There be many," says the psalmist, who speak this way.

But what does the distressed man say? "LORD, lift thou up the light of thy countenance upon us" (Ps. 4:6); and then adds in the next verse, "Thou hast put gladness in my heart"—namely, by the light of God's countenance, for that is the medicine for a broken heart. "Thou hast put gladness in my heart, more than in the time that their corn and their wine increased" (4:7).

A broken heart relishes pardon, and savors the consolations of the Holy Ghost. As a hungry and thirsty man values bread and water, so the broken in heart value and honor the things of the Lord Jesus. His flesh, His blood, His promise, and the light of His countenance are the only things sweet to the taste of the wounded in spirit. The full soul loathes the honeycomb; the unbroken despise the gospel; they do not savor the things of God.

If twenty men were to hear a pardon read, and only one of the twenty were condemned to death, which of these men would taste the sweetness of that pardon—the nineteen who are not condemned, or the one who was? The condemned man, of course. This is the case here. The broken in heart is a condemned man; a sense of condemnation, among other things, has indeed broken his heart; nothing but a sense of forgiveness can bind it up and heal it. But could he be healed if he could not truly taste and relish this forgiveness? No; forgiveness would be as much a stranger to him as it is to one who has no sense of his need for it.

So why do some so greatly value what others despise, since they both stand in need of the same grace and mercy of God in Christ? It is because the one sees his woeful, miserable state, and the other does not.

And thus have I showed you the necessity of a broken heart:

1. Man is dead, and must be quickened.
2. Man is a fool, and must be made wise.
3. Man is proud, and must be humbled.
4. Man is self-willed, and must be broken.
5. Man is fearless, and must be made to consider.
6. Man is a false believer, and must be rectified.
7. Man is a lover of sin, and must be weaned from it.
8. Man is wild, and must be tamed.
9. Man has no appetite for the things of God, and cannot delight in them, until his heart is broken.

5

Why a Broken Heart
Is Esteemed by God

And now I come next to the reasons why a broken heart, a heart truly contrite, is to God such an excellent thing. That it is excellent to Him we have proven by six demonstrations; what a broken heart is, we have shown by six signs; that the heart must be broken, is evident by the nine reasons given in the previous chapter; and why God esteems a broken heart to be an excellent thing will be shown by what follows.

First. A broken heart is *the handiwork of God*—a heart of His own preparing, for His own service, a sacrifice provided by Himself; as Abraham said, "God will provide himself a lamb" (Gen. 22:8).

This is why it is said, "The preparations of the heart in man . . . is from the LORD" (Prov. 16:1). And again, "God maketh my heart soft, and the Almighty troubleth me" (Job 23:16). The heart, which by nature is hard, senseless, and impenetrable, will remain so until God, as was said, bruises it with His hammer and melts it with His fire. The stony nature of it is therefore said to be taken away by God. "I will take away the stony heart out of your flesh, and I will give you an heart of flesh" (Ezek. 36:26). "I will take away the stony heart" (the stoniness or hardness of your heart) "and I will give you an heart of flesh"—that is, He will make your heart sensitive, soft, wieldable, governable, and penitent.

Sometimes God tells men to rend their hearts—not because they can, but to convince them that, though it must be so, they cannot do it; so he tells them to make themselves a new heart, and a new spirit, for the same reason; for if God does not rend it, it remains unrent; if God does not make it new, it remains an old one still. This is what is meant by His bending of men for Himself (see Zech. 9:13), and of His working in them that which is pleasing in His sight (Phil. 2:13).

The heart, soul, or spirit, in itself, as it came from God's fingers, is a precious thing, a thing in God's account worth more than all the world. This heart, soul, or spirit, sin has hardened, the devil has bewitched, the world has deceived. This heart, thus beguiled, God covets and desires: "My son," He says, "give me thine heart, and let thine eyes observe my ways" (Prov. 23:26).

Man cannot do this, for his heart has the mastery of him, and it does nothing but carry him into all sorts of futility. What now must be done? Why, God must take the heart by storm, by power, and bring it into compliance with the Word. But the heart of itself will not do it; it is deluded, captured by someone other than God.

So God now takes up His sword, brings down the heart with labor, opens it, and drives out the strong man that captured it; He wounds the heart and makes it sting for its rebellion, that it may cry; so He purifies it for Himself. "He maketh sore, and bindeth up: he woundeth, and his hands make whole" (Job 5:18). Thus having made it for Himself, it becomes His habitation, His dwelling place: "That Christ may dwell in your hearts by faith" (Eph. 3:17).

But I will not swerve from the subject at hand—that a broken heart is the handiwork of God, a sacrifice of His own preparing; a material fitted for Himself.

1. By breaking the heart He opens it, and makes it a receptacle for the graces of His Spirit—a storeroom in which, when unlocked, God puts the jewels of the gospel. There He puts His fear: "I will put my fear in their hearts" (Jer. 32:40); there He writes His law: "I will put my law in their inward parts, and write it in their hearts" (31:33); there He puts His Spirit: "I will put my Spirit within you" (Ezek. 36:27). The heart, I say, God chooses for His storeroom: there He hides His treasure; there is the seat of justice, mercy, and every grace of God—but only when it is broken, made contrite; and so regulated by the holy Word.

2. The heart, when broken, is like sweet spices when beaten; as spices cast their fragrant scent into the nostrils of men, so the heart when broken casts its sweet smells in the nostrils of God. The incense, which was a type of prayer of old, was to be beaten or bruised, and then burned in the censer. The heart must be beaten or bruised, and then the sweet scent will come

out—groans, and cries, and sighs for the mercy of God; these sounds are a very excellent thing to Him, and pleasing in His nostrils.

Second. A broken heart is in the sight of God an excellent thing because *it is submissive; it falls before God and gives Him glory*. All this is true from a multitude of scriptures, which I need not here mention. Hence such a heart is called an honest heart, a good heart, a perfect heart, a heart fearing God, and is sound in God's statutes.

Now, this is nothing less than an excellent thing, if we consider that such a heart yields unfeigned obedience to Him. "Ye have obeyed from the heart," says Paul to them at Rome, "that form of doctrine which was delivered you" (Rom. 6:17).

Unfortunately, the heart, before it is broken and made contrite, is of quite another temper: "It is not subject to the law of God, neither indeed can be" (8:7). The great struggle before the heart is broken is about who shall be Lord, God or the sinner. True, the right of dominion is the Lord's; but the sinner will not allow it, and asserts his own will, saying, "Who is lord over us?" (Ps. 12:4); they say to God, "We are lords, we will come no more unto thee" (Jer. 2:31).

This also is evident by their practice; no matter what God may say, they do what they want. "Keep my sabbath," says God; "I will not," says the sinner. "Leave your whoring," says God; "I will not," says the sinner. "Do not tell lies, nor swear, nor curse, nor blaspheme My holy name," says God; "Oh, but I will," says the sinner. "Turn to Me," says God; "I will not," says the sinner. "The right of dominion is mine," says God; but like the young rebel Adonijah, the sinner says, "I will be king" (1 Kings 1:5).

This is intolerable, insufferable—yet every sinner by practice says such things as this, for they have not submitted themselves to the righteousness of God.

There can be no concord, communion, agreement, or fellowship when there is enmity on one side and flaming justice on the other (see 2 Cor. 6:14–16; Zech 11:8). And what delight, contentment, or pleasure can God take in such men? None at all, though they may be in the company of the best saints of God; not even if the best of saints pray for them. This is why it says, "Then said the LORD unto me, Though Moses and Samuel stood before me"—that is, to pray for them—"yet my mind could not be toward this people: cast them out of my sight, and let them go forth" (Jer. 15:1).

There is nothing but open war, acts of hostility, and shameful rebellion on the sinner's side—and what delight can God take in that? Therefore, if God wants to bend and buckle the spirit of such a one, He must shoot an arrow at him, a barbed arrow, such as may not be plucked out of the wound: an arrow that will stick fast and cause the sinner to fall down as dead at God's feet (see Ps. 38:2). Only then will the sinner deliver up his arms, surrender himself as one conquered, and beg for the Lord's pardon. He will not do so till then, at least not sincerely.

And now God has overcome; "his right hand, and his holy arm, hath gotten him the victory" (98:1). Now He rides in triumph with His captive at His chariot wheel; now He glories; now the bells in heaven ring; now the angels shout for joy—yes, they are told to do so: "Rejoice with me, for I have found my sheep which was lost" (Luke 15:6). Now also the sinner, as a token of being overcome, lies grovelling at His feet, saying, "Thine arrows are sharp in the heart of the king's enemies, whereby the people fall under thee" (Ps. 45:5).

Now the sinner submits, now he follows his conqueror in chains, now he seeks peace, and would give all the world, were it his own, to be in the favor of God, and have any hope of being saved by Christ. This must be pleasing to God; it can be nothing but acceptable in God's sight. "A broken and a contrite heart, O God, thou wilt not despise" (Ps. 51:17). For it is the desire of His own heart, the work of His own hands.

Third. Another reason why a broken heart is such an excellent thing to God is this: *a broken heart prizes Christ, and has a high esteem for Him*. "They that are whole have no need of the physician, but they that are sick" (Mark 2:17). "They that are sick" are the brokenhearted; for God makes men sick by striking them, by breaking their hearts. So sickness and wounds are put together; the one is a true effect of the other (see Mic. 6:13; Hos. 5:13).

Can anyone think that God is pleased when men despise His Son, saying, "He hath no form nor comeliness; and when we shall see him, there is no beauty that we should desire him" (Isa. 53:2)? And yet those whose hearts God has not softened say this of Him; the elect themselves confess that before their hearts were broken, they despised Him also. He is, they say, "despised and rejected of men . . . and we hid as it were our faces from him; he was despised, and we esteemed him not" (Isa. 53:3).

He is indeed the great deliverer; but what is a deliverer to those who never saw themselves in bondage, as was said before? That is why it is said of him who delivered the city, "No man remembered that same poor man" (Eccl. 9:15).

He greatly suffered and was bruised for their transgressions, that they might not receive the punishment of hell, which by their sins they have earned for themselves. But what is that to them, who never saw anything but beauty, and never tasted anything but sweetness in sin?

He is the one who, by His intercession, holds back the hand of God, and who restrains Him from cutting off the drunkard, the liar, and unclean person, even when they are in the very act of their abominations; but their hard, stupefied heart has no sense of such kindness as this, so they take no notice of it. How many times has God said to this dresser of His vineyard, "Cut down the barren fig tree" (see Luke 13:7), while He, by His intercession, has prevailed for a reprieve for another year! But no notice is taken of this, no thanks is from them returned to Him for such kindness by Christ. Such ungrateful, unthankful, inconsiderate wretches as these must be a continual eyesore and a great provocation to God; and yet this is how men act before their hearts are broken (see Luke 13:6–9).

Christ, as I said, is called a physician; in fact, He is the only soul-physician. He heals, however desperate the disease; yes, and whoever He heals, He heals them forever. "I give unto them eternal life" (John 10:28), and He does it all at no cost, out of mere mercy and compassion.

But what is all this to one who does not see his sickness, his wound? What good is the best physician alive, or all the physicians in the world put together, to him who knows no sickness, who is aware of no disease? Physicians may go begging for all the healthy people. Physicians are of value only to those who are sick.

This is why Christ is so little valued in the world. God has not made them sick by striking them; His sword has not given them a wound; His dart has not been struck through their liver; they have not been broken with His hammer, nor melted with His fire. So they have no regard for Him as a physician; they think nothing of all the provision which God has made for the salvation of their souls.

But let such a soul be wounded, let such a heart be broken, let such a one be made sick through the sting of guilt, and be made to wallow in ashes under the burden of his transgressions—then he will say, "Who but Christ is the physician? Wash me, Lord; heal my wounds; pour Your wine and oil into my sore, Lord Jesus"; "Make me to hear joy and gladness; that the bones which thou hast broken may rejoice" (Ps. 51:8).

Nothing now is as welcome as healing, and no man as desirable as Christ. His name is the best of names, His love the best of loves; to such a soul, He is "the chiefest among ten thousand" (Song of Sol. 5:10).

As bread to the hungry, water to the thirsty, light to the blind, or liberty to the imprisoned, so, and a thousand times more, is Jesus Christ to the wounded and brokenhearted. Now, as was said, this must be excellent in God's eyes, since Christ Jesus is so glorious in His eyes. To treat with contempt what I count as excellent is offensive to me; but to value what I value is pleasing to me; such an opinion is excellent in my sight. What does Christ say? "The Father himself loveth you, because ye have loved me" (John 16:27). Whoever has a high esteem for Christ, the Father has a high esteem for them. Hence it is said, "He that acknowledgeth the Son hath the Father also" (1 John 2:23); the Father will be his, and will do for him as a Father, if he receives and honors His Son.

But no one but the brokenhearted will or can do this, because they, and they only, are aware of how desirable and worthy the Son is.

I dare to appeal to all the world as to the truth of this, and I say it again: the brokenhearted, and no one but them, have hearts of esteem in the sight of God. However, "the heart of the wicked is little worth" (Prov. 10:20), for it is destitute of a precious esteem of Christ, and cannot be anything but destitute, because it is not wounded, broken, and made aware of its need of His mercy.

Fourth. A broken heart is of great esteem with God, because *it is a thankful heart—thankful for the sense of sin and grace it has received.* The broken heart is a sensitive heart. This we touched upon before. It is sensitive to the dangers which sin leads to; yes, and has good reason to be sensitive, because it has seen and felt what sin is, both in the guilt and punishment that by law it deserves.

Just as a broken heart is sensitive to sin—its evil nature and consequences—so it is also sensitive to the fact that God will deliver the soul from the day of judgment. Consequently, it must be a thankful heart. "Whoso offereth praise glorifieth me" (Ps. 50:23), God says; and God loves to be glorified. God's glory is dear to Him; He will not part with it (see Isa. 42:8).

Since the brokenhearted is a sensitive soul, it follows that he is a thankful soul. "Bless the LORD, O my soul," said David, "and all that is within me, bless his holy name" (Ps. 103:1). What a blessing he bestows on God! And yet, not content with that, he goes on to say, "Bless the LORD, O my soul, and forget not all his benefits" (103:2). And what are these benefits? God is the one "Who forgiveth all thine iniquities; who healeth all thy diseases; Who redeemeth thy life from destruction; who crowneth thee with lovingkindness and tender mercies" (103:3–4).

But how did David come to know about these benefits? Why, he knew what it was to hang over the mouth of hell for sin; yes, he knew what it was for death and hell to beset and compass him about; yes, they took hold of him, as we have said, and were pulling of him down into the deep; he saw this to the breaking of his heart.

He also saw the way of life, and had his soul relieved with faith and a taste of that life—and that made him a thankful man. If a man with a broken leg is made to understand that breaking his leg kept him from breaking of his neck, he will be thankful to God for a broken leg. "It is good for me," said David, "that I have been afflicted" (Ps. 119:71). He was by that affliction preserved from great danger, for "Before I was afflicted I went astray" (119:67).

Who can be thankful for a mercy without being aware that they need it, have received it, and received it out of God's mercy? Now, the brokenhearted, the man that is of a contrite spirit, is aware of this, and aware that they are mercies of the best sort; therefore, he cannot help but be a thankful man, and have a heart esteemed by God, because it is a thankful heart.

Fifth. A broken heart is greatly esteemed as an excellent thing in the sight of God because *it is a heart that desires now to become a receptacle or habitation for the spirit and graces of the Spirit of God*. It was under the devil's control before, and was contented to be so. But now it desires to receive and be possessed by the Holy Spirit of God. "Create in me a clean heart," said David, "and renew a right spirit within me. . . . Take not thy holy spirit from me . . . and uphold me with thy free spirit" (Ps. 51:10–12). Now he desires a clean heart and a right spirit; now he desires the sanctifying of the blessed Spirit of grace— something which the uncircumcised in heart resist and despise (see Acts 7:51; Heb. 10:29).

A broken heart, therefore, is suited to the heart of God; a contrite spirit is one spirit with Him. God, as I said before, covets to dwell with the broken in heart, and the broken in heart desire communion with Him. Here, now, is an agreement, a oneness of mind; now "this [same] mind [is] in you, which was also in Christ Jesus" (Phil. 2:5). This certainly is an excellent spirit; this certainly is better to God, in His sight, than thousands of rams, or ten thousand rivers of oil. But does the carnal world covet such a spirit, and the blessed graces it enjoys? No, they despise it, as I said before; they mock it; they prefer to tolerate any sorry, dirty lust instead; and the reason is because they do not have a broken heart, that heart so highly esteemed by God, and because of that, they remain hostile to God.

The brokenhearted know that the sanctifying of the Spirit is a good means to avoid spiritual relapse, which no one can recover from unless his heart is wounded a second time. Doubtless David had a broken heart at first conversion, and if that brokenness had remained—that is, had he not given way to hardness of heart again— he never would have fallen into that sin out of which he could not be recovered, but by the breaking of his bones a second time. Therefore, I say, a broken heart is greatly esteemed by God; for it—and I will add, as long as it retains its tenderness—covets no one but God, and the things of His Holy Spirit; sin is an abomination to it.

6

Advantages of Keeping
Your Heart Tender

And before I go any further, this is a fit place to show you some of the advantages a Christian gets by keeping of his heart tender. For just as having a broken heart is an excellent thing, so keeping this broken heart tender is also very advantageous.

First. This is the way to always maintain in your soul *a fear of sinning against God*. Christians do not wink at or give way to sin until their hearts begin to lose their tenderness. A tender heart will be troubled by the sin of another, and more than that, afraid of committing that sin itself (see 2 Kings 22:19).

Second. A tender heart *quickly yields to prayer*—yes, is prompted to it, and puts an edge and fire into it. We are never delinquent in prayer until our heart has lost its tenderness— and then it grows cold, flat, and formal, and so we take a carnal approach to that holy duty.

Third. A tender heart *is always ready to repent* for the least fault or slip, the most fleeting sinful thought, it may be guilty of. In many things the best of us stumble; but if a Christian loses his tenderness, if he says he has to "seek" repentance, his heart has grown hard. He has lost that spirit, that kind spirit of repentance he used to have. Thus it was with the Corinthians; they were decayed, and lost their tenderness, and so their sin—yes, their great sins—remained unrepented of (see 2 Cor. 12:20).

Fourth. A tender heart *desires frequent communion with God*, while he who is hardened, though the seed of grace is in him, will be content to eat, drink, sleep, wake, and go days without number without Him (see Isa. 17:10; Jer. 2:32).

Fifth. A tender heart *is a wakeful, watchful heart*. It watches against sin in the soul, in the family, in the church, in spiritual duties and performances. It watches against Satan, the world, the flesh, etc. But when the heart is not tender, there is sleepiness, unwatchfulness, idleness—causing the heart, the family, and the church to be defiled, spotted, and blemished with sin; for a hard heart departs from God, and turns aside in all these things.

Sixth. A tender heart *will deny itself, even in lawful things*, will even refrain from that which is permissible to do, in case some Jew, or Gentile, or the church of God, or any member of it, should be offended or made weak because of it. The Christian who has lost his tenderness will not only refuse to deny himself in lawful things, but will even meddle in things utterly forbidden, regardless of who it may offend, grieve, or make weak. For an instance of this, we need go no further than David in our text, who, while he was tender, trembled at little things; but when his heart was hardened, he could take Bathsheba to satisfy his lust, and kill her husband to cover his wickedness.

Seventh. A tender heart—I mean, the heart kept tender—*avoids many blows, lashes, and fatherly chastisements* from the scourging hand of God, because it shuns the cause, which is sin.

"With the pure thou wilt show thyself pure; [but] with the froward thou wilt shew thyself unsavoury" (2 Sam. 22:27; see also Ps. 18:25–27).

Many needless rebukes and wounds happen to the saints of God through their unwise behavior. When I say needless, I mean they are only necessary to reclaim us from our futile ways; for we would not have to feel the pain of them were it not for our foolishness. Hence the afflicted is called a fool, because his folly brings his affliction upon him. "Fools," says David, "because of their transgression, and because of their iniquities, are afflicted" (107:17). And therefore, as was said before, he calls his sin his "foolishness" (38:5). And again, "[God] will speak peace unto his people, and to his saints: but let them not turn again to folly" (85:8). "If his children forsake my law . . . Then will I visit their transgression with the rod, and their iniquity with stripes" (89:30, 32).

How to Keep the Heart Tender

But what should a Christian do, when God has broken his heart, to keep it tender?

To this I will speak briefly. First, I will give you several cautions; second, several directions.

Several Cautions

1. Take heed not to choke out the conviction that is breaking your heart by trying to put out of your mind the cause of your conviction. Instead, nourish and cherish those things, deeply and soberly meditating on them. Think, therefore, to yourself, *What was it that first wounded my heart?* And keep that in mind until, by the grace of God and the redeeming blood of Christ, it is removed.

2. Shun foolish, worldly companions. Keeping company with fools has stifled many a conviction, killed many a desire, and made many a soul fall into hell, that once was in fierce pursuit of heaven. A companion that is not profitable to the soul is hurtful. "He that walketh with wise men shall be wise: but a companion of fools shall be destroyed" (Prov. 13:20).

3. Beware of idle talk, that you neither listen to nor join with it. "Go from the presence of a foolish man, when thou perceivest not in him the lips of knowledge" (Prov. 14:7). "Evil communications corrupt good manners" (1 Cor. 15:33), and "A fool's . . . lips are the snare of his soul" (Prov. 18:7). Therefore, beware of these things.

4. Beware of the least motivation to sin, that you do not tolerate it; tolerating the smallest of sins

makes way for bigger ones.[8] David's eye took his heart, and so his heart nourishing the thought, made way for the woman's company, the act of adultery, and bloody murder. "Take heed, brethren . . . lest any of you be hardened through the deceitfulness of sin" (Heb. 3:12–13). Remember that the one who wants to split a log drives the thin end of the wedge in first, and keeps driving until it does its work.

5. Beware of evil examples among the godly; don't let anyone teach you to do that which the Word of God forbids. Sometimes Satan makes use of a good man's bad ways, to spoil and harden the heart of them that come after. Peter's bad example could have spoiled Barnabas and several others. Therefore be cautious about following even good men's ways, and measure both theirs and your own by no other rule but the holy Word of God (Gal. 2:11–13).

6. Beware of unbelief, or atheistic thoughts; do not question of the truth and reality of heavenly things. Unbelief is the worst of evils; your heart cannot be tender if you nourish doubts in it. "Take heed, brethren, lest there be in any of you an evil heart of unbelief, in departing from the living God" (Heb. 3:12).

These necessary cautions should be observed with all diligence by anyone who, once their heart is made tender, wants to keep it so. And now we come to directions for keeping one's heart tender.

Several Directions

1. Labor after a deep knowledge of God to keep it warm upon thy heart; knowledge of His presence, that is everywhere. "Do not I fill heaven and earth, saith the LORD?" (Jer. 23:24).

   a. Knowledge of His piercing eye, running to and fro throughout the earth, beholding in every place the evil and the good (Prov. 15:3); that "his eyes behold, his eyelids try, the children of men" (Ps. 11:4).

   b. Knowledge of His power, that He is able to turn and dissolve heaven and earth into dust and ashes; and that they are in His hand but as a scroll or vesture (see Heb. 1:11–12).

   c. Knowledge of His justice, that the rebukes of it are as devouring fire (see Heb. 12:29).

   d. Knowledge of His faithfulness in fulfilling promises to them to whom they are made, and of His threatenings on the impenitent (see Matt. 5:18, 24:35; Mark 13:31).

2. Labor to get and keep a deep sense of sin in its evil nature, and in its soul-destroying effects upon thy heart; be persuaded, that it is the only

enemy of God, and that none hate, or are hated of God, but through that.

a. Remember it turned angels into devils, thrust them down from heaven to hell.

b. That it is the chain in which they are held and bound over to judgment (see 2 Pet. 2:4; Jude 6).

c. That it was for this that Adam was turned out of paradise; that the old world was drowned; that Sodom and Gomorrah were burned with fire from heaven; that cost Christ His blood to redeem you from its curse; and that it is the only thing that can keep you out of heaven for ever and ever.

d. Consider the pains of hell. Christ makes use of that as an argument to keep the heart tender; yes, to that end He repeats and repeats, and repeats, both the nature and durability of its burning flame, and of the gnawing of the never-dying worm that dwells there (Mark 9:43–48).

3. Consider death—both the certainty that you *will* die, and the uncertainty of *when*. "We must needs die" (2 Sam. 14:14); our days are determined—the number is known by God, though not by us (see Job 7:1, 14:1–5); we could not increase their number, even if we could give a

thousand worlds to do it. Consider that you must die but once—I mean but once as to this world; if you leave this world and do not die well, you can't come back again and die better. "It is appointed unto men once to die, but after this the judgment" (Heb. 9:27).

4. Consider also of the certainty and terribleness of the day of judgment, when Christ will sit on His great white throne, and the dead, at the sound of the trump of God, will be raised up; when the elements, with heaven and earth, shall melt and burn with fire; when Christ shall separate men one from another, as a shepherd divides the sheep from the goats; when the books shall be opened, the witnesses produced, and every man judged according to his works; when heaven's gate shall stand open to them that shall be saved, and the jaws of hell stand gaping for them that shall be damned (see Acts 5:30–31, 10:42; Matt. 25:31–32, 34, 46; Rev. 2:11; 1 Cor. 15:51; Rev. 20:12, 15; 2 Pet. 3:7, 10, 12; Rom. 2:2, 15, 16; Rev. 22:12).

5. Consider that Christ Jesus did not harden His heart against those sorrows He had to suffer to redeem your soul. Though He could have rightly and justly hardened His heart against you, because you had sinned against Him, He rather awakened Himself, and put on all pity,

compassion, and tender mercies. In His love and pity He saved us. His tender mercies from on high have visited us. He loved us, and gave Himself for us. Learn, then, from Christ, to be tender to yourself, and to endeavor to keep your heart tender toward God, to the salvation of your soul. But let us draw to a conclusion.

7

How God Uses a Broken Heart

Let us now, then, look at the uses God makes of a broken heart.

FIRST USE. The truth is that the those who truly come to God have had their hearts broken—their hearts are broken to cause them to come to Him. This shows that the link between sin and the soul is so firm, so strong, so inviolable, that nothing can break, disannul, or make it void unless the heart is broken. It was so with David—his new link with it could not be broken until his heart was broken.

It is amazing to consider what hold sin has on some men's souls, spirits, will, and affections. It is to them better than heaven, better than God, better than the soul, even better than salvation—this is evident because, though all these are offered to them on the sole condition that they simply leave their sins, they still choose to remain in their sins, to stand and fall by them.

What do you say to this, sinner? Isn't this true? How many times have you been offered heaven and salvation freely, if you would only break your bond with this great enemy of God, this great enemy of your soul? But you could never be brought to the point of breaking that bond—not by threatening nor by promise.

It is said of Ahab that he "did sell himself to work wickedness" (1 Kings 21:25); and in another place it says, "for your iniquities have ye sold yourselves" (Isa. 50:1). But what is this iniquity? Why, it is nothing, and a thousand times worse than nothing; but because nothing is, as we say, nought, therefore it goes under that term, where God said again to the people, "Ye have sold yourselves for nought" (52:3). But, I say, what an amazing thing is this, that a rational creature should make no better a bargain; that one that is so wise in all earthly things should be such a fool in the thing that is the most important. And yet, fool that he is, he tells every one he meets that he is one, because he will not break his bond with sin until his heart is broken. "Men loved darkness rather than light" (John 3:19). Yes, they make it clear that they love it, since even so great an offer will not persuade them to leave it.

SECOND USE. Is it not true that the man who truly comes to God for salvation has had his heart broken? If so, this shows us why some men's hearts are broken—even a reason why God breaks some men's hearts for sin: because He would not have them die in it, but rather come to God that they might be saved.

We can see in this, therefore, how God chooses to save some men's souls. He breaks their hearts, but He saves them; He kills them, that they may live; He wounds them, that He may heal them. And it seems by our discourse that now there is no way left but this; fair means, as we say, will not do; good words, a glorious gospel, begging and pleading with blood and tears, will not do. Men are resolved to press God to the limit. If He will have them, He must fetch them, follow them, catch them, lame them—yes, break their bones—or else He shall not save them.

Some men think an invitation, an outward call, a rational discourse, will do; but they are very deceived. A power, an exceeding great and mighty power, must attend the Word, or it does not work effectually to the salvation of the soul. I know these things (an invitation, a call, a discourse) are enough to leave men without excuse, but yet they are not enough to bring men home to God. Sin has a hold on them, they have sold themselves to it; the power of the devil has a hold on them, they are his captives to his will; yes, and more than all this, their will is one with sin, and with the devil, to be held captive by it: and if God gives not contrition, repentance, or a broken heart for sin, no one will have the motivation to forsake this horrible plot against their soul (see 2 Tim. 2:24–25).

This is why men who come, who are brought to Him, are said to be drawn to Him (see Isa. 26:9; John 6:44). No wonder that John says, "Behold, what manner of love the Father hath bestowed upon us" (1 John 3:1)! Here is cost bestowed, pains bestowed, labor bestowed, repentance bestowed; yes, and a heart made sore, wounded, broken, and filled with pain and sorrow, to lead to the salvation of the soul.

THIRD USE. This then may teach us what value to place upon a broken heart. A broken heart is what God esteems—what God counts better than all external service. A broken heart is needed for salvation, to come to Christ for life. The world does not know what to make of it, nor what to say to one who has a broken heart, and therefore they despise it, and consider the man that carries a broken heart in his bosom to be a moping fool, a miserable wretch, an undone soul. But "a broken and a contrite heart, O God, thou wilt not despise" (Ps. 51:17); a broken heart takes God's eye, God's heart: He chooses it for a companion; yes, God has told His Son to look favorably on such a man, and has promised him salvation, as has already been shown.

Sinner, have you obtained a broken heart? has God bestowed a contrite spirit upon you? He has given you what He Himself is pleased with; He has given you a storeroom to hold His grace in; He has given you a heart that can heartily desire His salvation, a heart after His own heart; that is, such as suits His mind. True, it is painful now, sorrowful now, penitent now, grieved now; now it is broken, now it bleeds, now it sobs, now it sighs, now it mourns and cries to God. Good, very good! All this is because He plans to make you laugh; He has made you sorry on earth that you might rejoice in heaven. "Blessed are they that mourn, for they shall be comforted. . . . Blessed are ye that weep now, for ye shall laugh" (Matt. 5:4; Luke 6:21).

But soul, be sure you have this broken heart. Not all hearts are broken hearts; nor is every heart that seems to have a wound a heart that is truly broken. A man may be cut, yet not cut to the heart; a man may have another heart, yet not a broken heart (see Acts 7:54; 1 Sam. 10:9). We know there is a difference between a wound in the flesh and a wound in the spirit; yes, a man's sin may be wounded, yet his heart not broken. Such was Pharaoh's, such was Saul's, such was Ahab's; but none of them had the mercy of a broken heart.

Therefore, I say, take heed; not every scratch with a pin, or prick with a thorn, or blow that God gives with His Word upon the heart of sinners, will break them. God gave Ahab such a blow that He made him stoop, fast, humble himself, gird himself with sackcloth, and lie in ashes, which was a great matter for a king; he went around meekly, yet he never had a broken heart (see 1 Kings 21:27, 29). What shall I say? Pharaoh and Saul confessed their sins, Judas repented himself of his doings, Esau sought the blessing, and that carefully with tears, and yet none of them had a heart rightly broken, or a spirit truly contrite. Pharaoh, Saul, and Judas, were Pharaoh, Saul, and Judas still; Esau was Esau still; there was no gracious change, no thorough turning to God, no unfeigned parting with their sins, no hearty flight for refuge to lay hold on the hope of glory, though they indeed had thus been touched (see Exod. 10:16; 1 Sam. 26:21; Matt. 27:3; Heb. 12:14–17).

The consideration of these things call aloud to us to take heed that we not accept as a broken and a contrite spirit that which will not be accepted as one at the day of death and judgment. Seeking soul, let me advise you not to be deceived about something of so great importance.

First. Go back to the beginning of this book and compare yourself with signs of a broken and contrite heart, which I have, according to the Word of God, given to you for that end; and deal with your soul impartially about them.

Second. It will be of great help to you if you are sincere about it, to take it upon yourself to search of the Word, especially where you read of the conversion of men, and see if *your* conversion has a good resemblance to theirs. But in this be careful that you do not compare yourself with those good folk whose conversion is not described, or whose broken heart is not mentioned in Scripture; for not all the saints in Scripture have their conversion—the manner and nature of it—recorded in detail.

Third. Consider what the true signs of repentance are, as laid down in Scripture; for that is the true effect of a broken heart and a wounded spirit (see Matt. 3:5–6; Luke 18:13, 19:8; Acts 2:37–40, 16:29–30, 19:18–19; 2 Cor. 7:8–11).

Fourth. Take into consideration how God has said that those He intends to save shall be in their spirits. For this, read these scriptures:

> They shall come with weeping, and with supplications will I lead them. (Jer. 31:9)

> In those days, and in that time . . . the children of Israel shall come, they and the children of Judah together, going and weeping: they shall go, and seek the LORD their God. They shall ask the way to Zion with their faces thitherward, saying, Come, and let us join ourselves to the LORD in a perpetual covenant that shall not be forgotten. (50:4–5)

And they that escape of you shall remember me among the nations whither they shall be carried captives, because I am broken with their whorish heart, which have departed from me, and with their eyes, which go a whoring after their idols: and they shall loathe themselves for the evils which they have committed in all their abominations. (Ezek. 6:9)

But they that escape of them shall escape, and shall be on the mountains like doves of the valleys, all of them mourning, every one for his iniquity. (7:16)

And there shall ye remember your ways, and all your doings, wherein ye have been defiled; and ye shall loathe yourselves in your own sight for all your evils that ye have committed. (20:43)

Then shall ye remember your own evil ways, and your doings that were not good, and shall loathe yourselves in your own sight for your iniquities and for your abominations. (36:31)

And I will pour upon the house of David, and upon the inhabitants of Jerusalem, the spirit of grace and of supplications: and they shall look upon me whom they have pierced, and they shall mourn for him, as one mourneth for his only son, and shall be in bitterness for him, as one that is in bitterness for his firstborn. (Zech. 12:10)

Now all these are the fruits of the Spirit of God, and of the heart, when it is broken: therefore, soul, take notice of them, and because these are texts by which God promises that those whom he saves shall have this heart, this spirit, and these holy effects in them; therefore consider again, and examine yourself, whether this is the state and condition of *your* soul.

And to be sure that you do it fully, consider yet again, and remember these five things:

1. Here is such a sense of sin, and its irksomeness, that it makes one not only abhor sin, but also himself, because of his sin; it is worth your taking note of this.

2. Here is not only a self-abhorrence, but a sorrowful kind of mourning to God, at the consideration that the soul by sin has affronted, shown contempt for, disregarded, and treated as of no account both God and His holy Word.

3. Here are prayers and tears for mercy, with desires to be now out of love with sin forever,

and to be in heart and soul firmly joined and knit to God.

4. The people spoken of in these scriptures have scattered with tears and prayers, with weeping and supplication, all the way from Satan to God, from sin to grace, from death to life; they shall go weeping, and seeking the Lord their God.

5. These people, as strangers and pilgrims do, are not ashamed to ask of those they meet the way to Zion, the heavenly country; in this way they confess their honest ignorance, and their desire to know the way to life. Yes, by this they declare that there is nothing in this world, under the sun, or this side of heaven that can satisfy the longings, desires, and cravings of a broken and a contrite spirit. Be advised, and consider these things seriously, and compare your soul with them, and with whatever else you find here written for your conviction and instruction.

FOURTH USE. If a broken heart and a contrite spirit are of such esteem with God, it should encourage those who have it to come to God with it. I know there is great encouragement for men to come to God, for there is "one mediator between God and men, the man Christ Jesus"

(1 Tim. 2:5). This, I say, is the great encouragement, and nothing can take its place; but there are other encouragements subordinate to that, and a broken and a contrite spirit is one of them. This is evident from several places in Scripture.

Therefore, if you carry a broken heart and a sorrowful spirit within you, go to God and tell Him your heart is wounded, that you have sorrow in your heart, and you are sorry for your sins; but be careful not to lie about it.[9] Confess your sins to Him, and tell Him they are continually before you. David made an argument of these things, when he went to God by prayer. "O LORD," he said, "rebuke me not in thy wrath: neither chasten me in thy hot displeasure" (Ps. 38:1). But why did he do so? He says,

> Thine arrows stick fast in me, and thy hand presseth me sore. There is no soundness in my flesh, because of thine anger; neither is there any rest in my bones, because of my sin. For mine iniquities are gone over mine head: as a heavy burden they are too heavy for me. My wounds stink, and are corrupt, because of my foolishness. I am troubled; I am bowed down greatly; I go mourning all the day long. For my loins are filled with a loathsome disease: and there is no soundness

in my flesh. I am feeble and sore broken: I have roared by reason of the disquietness of my heart. Lord, all my desire is before thee; and my groaning is not hid from thee. My heart panteth, my strength faileth me: as for the light for mine eyes, it also is gone from me. My lovers and my friends stand aloof from my sore. (Ps. 38:2–11)

These are the words, sighs, complaints, prayers, and arguments of a broken heart to God for mercy; and so are these:

Have mercy upon me, O God, according to thy loving kindness: according unto the multitude of thy tender mercies blot out my transgressions. Wash me thoroughly from mine iniquity, and cleanse me from my sin. For I acknowledge my transgressions; and my sin is ever before me. (51:1–3)

God allows poor creatures who can, without lying, thus to plead and argue with Him. "I am poor and sorrowful," said the good man to him, "let thy salvation, O God, set me up on high" (69:29). Therefore, if you have a broken heart, God bids you to take courage, and say to your soul, "Why art thou cast down, O my soul?" as the brokenhearted usually are. "And why art thou disquieted within me? Hope thou in God"

(Ps. 42:11). "I had fainted," if I had not been of good courage; therefore, "be of good courage, and he shall strengthen thine heart" (27:13–14).

But the brokenhearted are far off from this; they faint; they reckon themselves among the dead; they think God will remember them no more: the thoughts of the greatness of God, of His holiness, and of their own sins and vileness, will certainly consume them. They feel guilt and anguish of soul; they go mourning all the day long; their mouth is full of gravel and bitterness, and they are made to drink wormwood and gall. And so one must be an expert indeed at believing, to come to God under such guilt and horror, and plead in faith that "the sacrifices of God are a broken spirit," such as he has; and that "a broken and a contrite heart, O God, thou wilt not despise" (51:17).

FIFTH USE. If a broken heart and a contrite spirit is of such esteem with God, then why should some be, as they are, so afraid of a broken heart, and so shy of a contrite spirit?

I have observed that some men are as afraid of a broken heart, or that they for their sins should have their hearts broken, as the dog is of the whip. They cannot stand the kind of books, sermons, preachers, or talk that tend to make a person aware of his sin, that break his heart and make him contrite for his sins. And so they heap to themselves such teachers, get such books, love such company, and delight in such discourse, as tends to harden rather than soften; as makes one desperate in, than sorrowful for, their sin. They say to such sermons, books, and preachers, as Amaziah said unto Amos, "O thou seer, go, flee thee away into the land of Judah, and there eat bread, and prophesy there, but prophesy not again any more at Bethel; for it is the king's chapel, and it is the king's court" (Amos 7:12–13).

Do these people realize what they are doing? Yes, or so they think; for heartbreaking preachers, books, and discourses tend to make one melancholy or mad; they make us so that we cannot take pleasure in ourselves, in our concerns, in our lives.

But, O ingrained[10] fool! Let me ask you, is it a time to take pleasure, and to amuse yourself, before you have mourned and been sorry for your sins? The mirth that is before repentance for sin will certainly end in heaviness.

That is why the wise man, putting both together, says that mourning must be first. There is "a time to weep, and a time to laugh; a time to mourn, and a time to dance" (Eccl. 3:4)—but what does an unconverted man have to laugh about? If you saw someone singing merry songs while being taken from Newgate Prison to Tyburn[11] to be hanged for felony, what would you think? Would you not consider him to be beside himself—or worse? And yet it is the same with him that is filled with mirth while he stands condemned by the Word of God for his trespasses. He has cause to mourn instead; yes, and he must mourn if he is ever to be saved.

Therefore my advice is, that instead of shunning books, preachers, and discourses that tend to make one aware of sin, and to break one's heart for it, one should covet them; for no one will ever be as he should—be concerned about or seek the salvation of his own soul—before he has a broken heart and a contrite spirit.

So don't be afraid of a broken heart; don't be shy about a contrite spirit. It is one of the greatest mercies that God bestows on a person. The heart rightly broken at the sense of sin, and made truly contrite for transgression, is a certain forerunner of salvation. This is evident from those six demonstrations which were laid down earlier to prove the point.

And let me awaken you to this truth: you must have your heart broken, whether you want to or not. God is resolved to break ALL hearts for sin at some time or another. Can it be imagined, sin being what it is, and God being who He is—to wit, a revenger of disobedience—but that at one time or another man must feel pain for sin? He mus feel pain, either in repentance or in condemnation. Whoever does not mourn for sin now, while the door of mercy is open, will mourn for sin later, when the door is shut.

Shall men despise God, break His law, have contempt for His threats, abuse His grace? Shut their eyes when He says, "See"? Stop their ears when He says, "Hear"? And shall they so escape? No—because He called, and they refused; He stretched out his hand, and they had no regard for it; therefore calamity will come upon them, as upon one in travail. Then they will cry in their distress, but God will laugh at their destruction, and mock when their fear comes (see Prov. 1:24–28).

I have often observed that the following warning is repeated at least seven times in the New Testament: "There shall be weeping and gnashing of teeth" (Matt. 8:12, 22:13, 24:51, 25:30; Luke 13:28) and "there shall be wailing and gnashing of teeth" (Matt. 8:12, 13:42, 50). Where? In hell, and at the bar of Christ's tribunal, when He comes to judge the world, and shuts the door to keep them out of glory—those who have on earth despised His offer of grace and overlooked the day of His patience. "There shall be wailing and gnashing of teeth"—they shall weep and wail over this.

There are but two more scriptures that I will mention, and then I will draw to a conclusion.

One is in Proverbs, where Solomon counsels young men to beware of "strange women"—that is, of wanton, ensnaring women. Take heed of them, he says, lest "thou mourn at the last"—that is, in hell, when you are dead—"when thy flesh and thy body are consumed, and say, How have I hated instruction, and my heart despised reproof, and have not obeyed the voice of my teachers, nor inclined mine ears to them that instructed me!" (Prov. 5:11–13).

The other scripture is in Isaiah, where he says,

> Because when I called, ye did not answer; when I spake, ye did not hear; but did evil before mine eyes, and did choose that

wherein I delighted not. Therefore thus saith the Lord God, Behold, my servants shall eat, but ye shall be hungry; behold, my servants shall drink, but ye shall be thirsty; behold, my servants shall rejoice, but ye shall be ashamed; behold, my servants shall sing for joy of heart, but ye shall cry for sorrow of heart, and shall howl for vexation of spirit. (Isa. 65:12–14)

How many "beholds" are here! and every "behold" is not only a call to careless ones to consider, but as a declaration from heaven that thus at last it shall be with all impenitent sinners—when others sing for joy in the kingdom of heaven, they shall sorrow in hell, and howl in vexation of spirit there.

So let me advise you not to be afraid of, but instead to covet a broken heart, and prize a contrite spirit! Covet it now, while the white flag is hung out; now, while the golden scepter of grace is held forth to you. Better to mourn now, when God inclines to mercy and pardon, than to mourn when the door is quite shut up. And take notice, that this is not the first time that I have given you this advice.

SIXTH USE. Lastly, If a broken heart be a thing of so great esteem with God as has been said, and if duties cannot be rightly performed by a heart that has not been broken, then this shows the vanity of those peoples' minds, and also the emptiness of their pretended "divine" services, who worship God with a heart that was never broken, and without a contrite spirit.

There has, indeed, at all times been great flocks of such professors in the world in every age, but to little purpose except to deceive themselves, mock God, and lay stumbling blocks in the way of others. A man whose heart was never truly broken, and whose spirit was never contrite, cannot profess Christ in earnest, cannot love his own soul in earnest; I mean, he cannot do these things in truth, and seek his own good the right way, for he lacks a foundation for it, that is, a broken heart for sin, and a contrite spirit.

That which makes a man a hearty, unfeigned, sincere seeker after the good of his own soul, is a sense of sin, and a godly fear of being overtaken by the danger it brings a man into. This makes him contrite or repentant, and puts him upon seeking of Christ the Savior, with heart-aching and heartbreaking considerations.

But this sincere seeking is impossible when this sense of sin, this godly fear, and this holy contrition is lacking. Professed seekers may make noises of repentence—the empty barrel makes the biggest sound—but test them, and they are full of air, full of emptiness, and that is all.

Such professors do not show concern for God's name or give credit to the gospel they profess; nor can they, for they lack what should obligate them to do so—a sense of pardon and forgiveness, by which their broken hearts have been replenished, relieved, and made to hope in God. Paul said the love of Christ constrained him. But what was Paul but a brokenhearted and contrite sinner (see Acts 9:3–6; 2 Cor. 5:14)?

When God shows a man the sin he has committed, the hell he has deserved, the heaven he has lost; and yet that Christ, and grace, and pardon may be had; it will make him serious, make him melt, break his heart. It will show him that there is more than air, more than a noise, more than an empty sound in religion; and this is the man whose heart, whose life, whose conversation, and all, will be engaged in the matters of the eternal salvation of his precious and immortal soul.

8

Objections Answered

Objection #1: Some may object that my words seem too rigid and overly critical; that, unless I moderate my statements, I could discourage many an honest soul.

My answer: I would not change a jot. Not an honest soul in all the world will be offended at my words; for no one can be an honest soul, I mean with reference to its concerns in another world, who has not had a broken heart, who never had a contrite spirit.

I will concede, because I want to be rightly understood, that not all brokenhearted people get into the same degree of trouble, nor lie so long under it, as some of their brethren do. But to go to heaven without a broken heart, or to be forgiven sin without a contrite spirit, is not what I believe. We speak not now of what is secret; revealed things "belong to us and to our children" (Deut. 29:29); nor must we venture to go further in our faith. Does not Christ say, "Those who are whole have no need of a physician" (see Matt. 8:12; Mark 2:17; Luke 5:31)? That is, they see no need, but Christ will make them see their need before He ministers His sovereign grace to them. And for good reason—otherwise, He will have but little thanks for His kindness.

Objection #2: But there are those that are godly educated from their childhood, and so drink in the principles of Christianity they know not how.

My answer: I count it one thing to receive the faith of Christ from men only, and another to receive it from God by the right means. If you are taught by an angel, yet not by God, you will never come to Christ. I do not say you will never profess Him. But if God speaks, and you hear and understand Him, that Voice will make such a work within you as was never made before. The voice of God is a voice by itself, and is so distinguished by them that are taught thereby (see John 6:44–45; Ps. 29; Hab. 3:12–16; Eph. 4:20–21; 1 Pet. 2:2–3).

Objection #3: But some men are not so debauched and profane as some, and so do not need to be as hammered and fired as others; they are not as broken and wounded as others.

My answer: God knows best what we need. Paul was as righteous before conversion as anyone who can pretend to it today, I suppose; yet despite that, he was made to shake, and was astonished at himself at his conversion. I truly think that the more righteous anyone is in his own eyes before conversion, the more need he has of heartbreaking work in order to be saved. A man is not by nature so easily convinced that his righteousness is just as abominable to God as his debauchery and profaneness.

A man's goodness is that which blinds him the most, is dearest to him, and is not easily parted with. Therefore, when one who thinks his own goodness is enough to commend him in whole or in part to God, is converted (and few such are converted), a great deal of breaking work upon his heart is required to make him come to Paul's conclusion, "What then? are we better than they? No, in no wise" (Rom. 3:9). He must be brought to see that his glorious robes are filthy rags, and his gainful things but loss and dung (see Isa. 64:6; Phil. 3).

This is also gathered from these words: "The publicans and the harlots go into the kingdom of God before [the Pharisees]" (Matt. 21:31). Why before them? But because they more readily hear the Word, are easier convinced of their need of Christ, and so are brought home to Him without, as I may say, all the trouble the Holy Ghost goes to to bring a Pharisee home to Him.

It is true that nothing is hard or difficult for God. But I speak after the manner of men. And if one takes to task a man debauched in this life, and one that is not so, and tries to convince them both that they are in a state of condemnation by nature, you will see that the Pharisee makes his appeals to God with, "God, I thank thee, that I am not as other men are"; while the publican hangs his head, shakes at heart, and smites upon his breast, saying, "God be merciful to me a sinner" (Luke 18:11, 13).

A self-righteous man is but a painted Satan, or a devil in fine clothes; but does he think this of himself? No! He says to others, "Stand by thyself, come not near to me; for I am holier than thou" (Isa. 65:5).

It is almost impossible for a self-righteous man to be saved. But He who can drive a camel through the eye of a needle can cause even the self-righteous to see his lost condition, and that he needs the righteousness of God, which is by faith in Jesus Christ. He can make him see that his own goodness stands more in his way to the kingdom of heaven than he was aware of. He can also make him realize that leaning on his own righteousness is as great an iniquity as any immorality that men commit.

To sum it up, those who are converted to God by Christ through the Word and Spirit— for this is what effectual conversion is—must have their hearts broken, and spirits made contrite; I say, it MUST be so, for the reasons showed before. Yes, and all decayed, apostatized, and backslidden Christians must, in order to return again to God, have their hearts broken, their souls wounded, their spirits made contrite, and be made sorry for their sins.

And so conversion to God is not as easy and as smooth a thing as some would have us believe. Why is man's heart compared to fallow ground,

God's Word to a plough, and his ministers to ploughmen, if the heart indeed has no need to be broken in order to receive the seed of God unto eternal life (Jer. 4:3; Luke 9:62; 1 Cor. 9:10)? Who does not know that fallow ground has to be ploughed before the farmer plants his seed? Yes, and after that the plowed ground often has to be soundly harrowed [smoothed out], or else he will have but a slender harvest.

Why is the conversion of the soul compared to grafting a tree, if it could be done without cutting? The Word is the graft, the soul is the tree, and the Word, as the graft, must be joined in by a wound; just to be stuck on the outside, or be tied on with a string, will do no good here. Heart must be set to heart, or your ingrafting will come to nothing (see Rom. 11:17, 24; Jer. 2:21).

Heartwood must be set to heartwood, and bark set to bark, or the sap will not be conveyed from the root to the branch; it must be done by means of a wound. The Lord opened the heart of Lydia, as a person opens the tree to graft in the branch, and so the Word was let into her soul. Then the Word and her heart cemented together, and became one (see Acts 16:14).

Why is Christ told to gird His sword upon
His thigh? Why must He make His arrows sharp,
that the heart may be shot, wounded, and made
to bleed? Why is He commanded to let it be so,
if the people would bow and fall kindly under
Him, and heartily implore His grace without
it (see Ps. 45:5; 55:3–4)? Because men are too
lofty, too proud, too wild, too devilishly resolved
in the ways of their own destruction. In their
behavior, they are like wild donkeys upon wild
mountains; nothing can break them of their
purposes, or hinder them from ruining their own
precious and immortal souls, but the breaking
of their hearts.

Why is a broken heart and a contrite spirit
put in place of all sacrifices we can offer to God?
You can see that this is so, if you compare Psalm
51:17 with the previous verse: "For thou desirest
not sacrifice; else would I give it: thou delightest
not in burnt offering." Why is it counted better
than all external parts of worship—all of them
put together? Could *anything* be able to make
a man a rightly made new creature without it?
"A broken heart, a contrite spirit, God will not
despise"; but you and all your works He will
certainly despise and reject if, when you come

to Him, you do not have a broken heart. Here, then, is the point: Come broken, come contrite, come aware of and sorry for your sins, or your coming will be counted as not coming to God in the right way, and you will consequently get no benefit from it.

Editor's Notes

1. This is beautifully and most impressively described in *The Pilgrim's Progress*, when the bitter feelings of poor Christian under convictions of sin, alarm his family and put it quite "out of order."

2. No one could speak more feelingly upon this subject than our author. He had been in deep waters, in soul-harrowing fear, while his heart—hard by nature—was under the hammer of the Word: "My soul was like a broken vessel. O, the unthought of imaginations, frights, fears, and terrors, that are affected by a thorough application of guilt, yielded to desperation!" (*Grace Abounding to the Chief of Sinners*, No. 186). Like the man that had his dwelling among the tombs.

3. The Christian, if he thinks of possessing "good motions" (i.e., stirrings of the heart), joins with such thoughts his inability to carry them into effect. "When I would do good, evil is present with me" (Rom. 7:21). How different is this to the self-righteous Ignorance, so vividly pictured in *The Pilgrim's Progress*:

   > Ignor.—I am always full of good motions that come into my mind, to comfort me as I walk.
   >
   > Chris.—What good motions? pray tell us.
   >
   > Ignor.—Why, I think of God and heaven.
   >
   > Chris.—So do the devils and damned souls!

   The whole of that deeply interesting dialogue illustrates the difficulty of self-knowledge, which can only be acquired by the teaching of the Holy Spirit.

4. This is in exact agreement with the author's experience, which he had published twenty-two years before, under the title of *Grace Abounding to the Chief of Sinners*:

> I was more loathsome in my own eyes than was a toad, and I thought I was so in God's eyes too. Sin and corruption, I said, would as naturally bubble out of my heart as water would out of a fountain. I thought that none but the devil himself could equal me for inward wickedness and pollution of mind.

A sure sign that God, as his heavenly Father, was enlightening his memory by the Holy Spirit.

5. "Christ and a crust" is the common saying to express the sentiment that Christ is all in all. The pitcher refers to the custom of pilgrims in carrying at their belt a vessel to hold water, and their staff having a crook by which it was dipped up from a well or river.

This account of the author's interview with a pious, humble woman is an agreeable episode which relieves the mind without diverting it from the serious object of the treatise. It was probably an event which took place in one of those pastoral visits which Bunyan was in the habit of making, and which, if wisely made, so endears a minister to the people of his charge.

6. However hard, and even harsh, these terms may appear, they are fully justified; and with all the author's great ability and renown, he has the grace of humility to acknowledge that, by nature and practice, he had been the biggest of fools.

7. Man must be burnt out of the stronghold in which he trusted: "Saved, yet so as by fire" (1 Cor. 3:15); "he shall baptize you with the Holy Ghost, and with fire" (Matt. 3:11, Luke 3:16); "is not my word like as a fire?" (Jer. 23:29). The work of regeneration and purification is a trying work; may the reader inquire, *Has this fire burnt up my wood, hay, and stubble?*

8. "Sin will at first, just like a beggar, crave / One penny or one halfpenny to have; / And if you grant its first suit, 'twill aspire / From pence to pounds, and so will still mount higher / To the whole soul!" —Bunyan's "Caution Against Sin" (poem).

9. This is faithful counsel. How many millions of lies are told to the all-seeing God, with unblushing effrontery, every Lord's Day—when the unconcerned and careless, or the saint of God, happy, most happy in the enjoyment of divine love, are led to say, "Have mercy upon us miserable sinners."

10. "Ingrained" is a term used in dyeing, when the raw material is dyed before being spun or woven; the color thus takes every grain, and becomes indelible. So with sin and folly; it enters every grain of human nature.

11. The frightful exhibition of parading a criminal from Newgate to Tyburn to be executed, was a common occurrence until the reign of George III, when so many were put to death that it was found handier for the wholesale butchery to take place at Newgate, by a new scaffold, in which twenty or thirty could be hung at once! When will such brutal exhibitions cease?

PUBLICATIONS

Fort Washington, PA 19034

This book is published by CLC Publications, an outreach of CLC Ministries International. The purpose of CLC is to make evangelical Christian literature available to all nations so that people may come to faith and maturity in the Lord Jesus Christ. We hope this book has been life changing and has enriched your walk with God through the work of the Holy Spirit. If you would like to know more about CLC, we invite you to visit our website:

www.clcusa.org

To know more about the remarkable story of the founding
of CLC International we encourage you to read

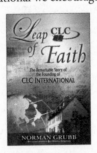

LEAP OF FAITH

Norman Grubb

Paperback
Size 5¹/₄ x 8, Pages 248
ISBN: 978-0-87508-650-7
ISBN (e-book): 978-1-61958-055-8